COARSE · SEA & FLY
FISHING

COARSE · SEA & FLY
FISHING

EDITED BY LEN CACUTT

NEW BURLINGTON BOOKS

A QUINTET BOOK

Published by New Burlington Books
6 Blundell Street
London N7 9BH

ISBN 1-85348-252-8

This book was designed and produced by
Quintet Publishing Limited
6 Blundell Street
London N7 9BH

Creative Director: Peter Bridgewater
Designers: Neal Cobourne, Annie Moss
Project Editor: Len Cacutt
Editor: Lindsay Porter

Typeset in Great Britain by
Central Southern Typesetters, Eastbourne
Manufactured in Hong Kong by Regent
Publishing Services Limited
Printed in Hong Kong

Some of the material in this publication
previously appeared in *Fly Fishing*,
Introduction to Fly Tying and *North American
Saltwater Fishing*

CONTENTS

INTRODUCTION: WHAT IS FISHING?   6

COARSE FISHING   16
THE COARSE FISH SPECIES   26
METHODS OF COARSE FISHING   38
COARSE FISHING WATERS   44
COARSE FISHING BAITS   50
ACCESSORIES   58

FLY FISHING   64
FLY FISHING TACKLE   65
PUTTING IT ALL TOGETHER   74
THE FLY FISHERMAN'S FISH SPECIES   81
THE WATERS WE FISH   83
FLY TYING   94
THE ESSENTIALS   97
PROPORTIONS   99
TECHNIQUES   101
MAKING YOUR FIRST FLY   105
ADDITIONAL MATERIALS IN COMMON USAGE   108
STANDARD WET FLIES   111
LURES   117
NYMPHS   124
DRY FLIES   130

SEA FISHING   136
SEA TACKLE   138
THE SEA ANGLER'S FISH SPECIES   149
SEA ANGLING BAITS   168
OFF-SHORE SEA FISHING   177
FISHING FROM THE SHORE   184
ACCESSORIES   192
BIG GAME FISHING   196

INDEX   **204**

INTRODUCTION

What is Fishing?

Perhaps the question should be 'What do anglers see in fishing?' because the word 'fishing' speaks for itself. It is the removal by man or other animal of a fish from its natural habitat. When fishing – or angling – as a sport or pastime is discussed it is the sporting fisherman with whom we are concerned. The angler seeks the fish with rod or line and at the business end of that line will be a baited hook, artificial fly or lure of some kind. From the US we have come to be familiar with the description of 'sportfisherman', but perhaps in order to avoid any accusation of sexism we should prefer, simply, 'sportfisher'.

We will disregard the eager toddler, bright-eyed and excited, armed with a long bamboo cane with its small metal-rimmed net, dabbling into the waters of a local pond for the pugnacious stickleback. This small fish's bristling dorsal spines and its eager darting to and fro in a small domestic aquarium is entertaining but our young, budding angler should be urged to return the stickleback to its natural habitat as soon as possible. It is never too young to be introduced to the proper care and consideration of the world's animal life. Sadly, the list of threatened species is growing.

Fishing is the archetypal, pleasurable get-away-from-it-all pastime and when taken to the extreme the beckoning finger of a limpid carp pool on a summer's evening, or the sound and sight of a beautiful beach where bass are going to be patrolling just beyond the near breakers, or the dimpling and heaving as trout rise to a mayfly hatch – any of these can tempt an angler away from his warm winter's bed, the cosy fireside, the gardening, even the Sunday lunch.

As with many of the good things of life, fishing can become an obsession and once one has been bitten by the 'angling bug' there is a danger of the loss to normal society of the fortunate, but afflicted angler smitten by the lure and challenge of the fishes. However, the sport has far more pluses than minuses. Perhaps most importantly it teaches respect and regard for the countryside and its animal life in and out of water. In addition, its soothing balm of gentle breeze, or chuckling stream; the endless regiment of the sea's waves gently rocking an anchored boat; the living spring of a well-worked fly rod and the beauty of its fly line as it curves gracefully out to settle light as thistledown in the path of a feeding trout — are all part and parcel of the way of life chosen by the sportfisher.

The reader new to this sport should not confuse the words 'fishing' and 'catching fish', the terms only become synonymous when in close context. But there is 'fishing' and *not catching fish*, something that can still be hugely enjoyable simply from the satisfaction the angler gets from his surroundings and his use of the tools of the trade. 'A good day's fishing' can, very surprisingly, describe a session when the fish ignored every bait and lure the angler tried. But while the angler's offerings remained ignored the peace and quiet of country or sea were seeping into the angler's body and mind and taking the place of everyday worry and irritation.

It has often been said that while the true fisherman obviously likes to return home with tales of the scaly monster he has dreamed about and now caught, he will be perfectly happy and relaxed after watching his float, his fly line, and his sea-rod tip stay unmoving from the moment his bait entered the water until he wound in as the sun set. He will insist that even though he caught nothing he was fishing, mentally prepared for the quiver, the pull, that mere suggestion of a twitch which says his offering was under investigation down there beneath the water's surface. It might be barely a rod's length away, on the other hand it could be in 40 fathoms of cold and darkness on the seabed.

ABOVE A fine day on the River Witham, Lincs, not too hot, perhaps a friend not too close, the river in good fettle, a recipe for pleasure.

OPPOSITE Depending on the species sought, winter fishing can be quite rewarding, especially for trout in spring-fed streams that stay somewhat warmer through the cold weather.

Anglers often seem to develop some strange ESP-like sense, as if being so close to nature triggers primaeval abilities which our cosseted, comfortable lives have diminished. Like the creatures which become alarmed before an earth-quake strikes, anglers instincts seem tuned into signals the human nervous system can no longer detect, and before any sign is recognized by man, some fishermen know that things are about to happen down there out of sight. I have personal experience of sitting in a rocking, gyrating boat well out of sight of land, and without any warning suddenly knowing – *knowing* – that action was about to begin. And it did, time and time again. My concentration suddenly doubled, I pre-pared for a strike – then suddenly the line tugged at the rod tip, the ratchet on the reel spool began to click as something pulled at the line, and the fish was on. What is it that triggers off the angler's alarm bells when up to that moment his tackle has given no indication, or signal? Something does, that's for sure! It is in the same category as a dog barking as you approach a house, long before any sign of your presence is noted by the people inside.

From a sporting point of view, fishing can lay claim to not a few generalisations: it is open to both sexes, the old and young, the vibrant and healthy, and the ailing or disabled. I have seen sightless anglers sitting round a lake, their ultra-sensitive finger-tips resting lightly on the line running through the rod-rings, their concentration total, waiting for that tiny *something* which heralds a bite. Their sighted assistants very often have little to do except net the fish and re-bait the hook.

As a sport, fishing has a far longer history than the original Greek Olympics. In Palaeolithic times, fishing was done for food, and we have many flint, bone and spine hooks as evidence. The modern fishing hook is different from the prehistoric models only in their advanced metallurgy. When they were not at war, the Assyrians of 3000 BC fished with a handline, and 2000-year-old Egyptian tomb paintings show those Dynastic ancients boat-fishing with rod and line. Chalres Chenevix Trench recorded that one bait Egyptian anglers used was a live rat.

It would be a brave, dedicated angler who would consider taking a box of live, squealing *Rattus norvegicus* to the waterside for his livebaiting session for pike. But who knows, there are those who can take a firm hold between finger and thumb of large black slugs and impale them on a hook without a trace of squeamishness. Chub are particularly fond of the largest, blackest slug. One chub specialist friend of mine, Charles Landells, keeps a well-stocked 'sluggery' at the back of his garden – and takes the biggest 'for a walk' before popping it into the bait tin before going fishing.

For many anglers, their sport is a form of escapism, not from shopping or one's accepted domestic duties, but from today's hectic commercial lifestyles, the pressures of business, the demands of the VAT-man, the Income Tax form,

ABOVE Tackle of twenty and more years ago: rod of split-cane, a Nottingham reel in mahogany, silk line, a pike float – and a fat pike.

TOP RIGHT Contented angler by a quiet lake in the heart of Surrey at Newdigate. Not a fishery full of specimens but a truly peaceful, delightful place in which to relax.

and of bureaucracy run wild. Few of us are fortunate enough to earn a living doing something we find easy and interesting as well as profitable. Fishing is not running away from life's domestic and commercial responsibilities; it is a very successful means of spending time pleasurably while recharging the human batteries so that domestic and work problems can be faced with renewed determination.

When at long last peace broke out at the end of World War II, angling in Great Britain, which had of necessity been abandoned for nearly five years, was suddenly transformed. Before, quiet men sat along riversides, canal towpaths and lake margins in studied contemplation of a green-and-red-painted float below which was hanging a worm or maggots on a hook. Sea-anglers, who always lived by or close to the sea, fished with thick, unyielding rods upon which were mounted great wooden centrepin reels (the origin of the hated 'block-and-tackle' smear aimed at sea fishing). Once the war was over and the soldiers, sailors, and airmen were disbanding, men were relieved of the horrors and dangers of combat, shrugging off the constrictions of barrack-square discipline and uniform. They were remembering that there was life before one had to fight for it and they were savouring their

ABOVE These cod and pollack will go in the fridge for a future meal, but not all do. Anglers must be in the forefront of conservation of all fish species.

OPPOSITE This superb dab was caught at Chesil Beach, Dorset. Often a photograph is the only remaining record of a prize catch which is later returned to the water.

new-found freedom, a time when they could go pretty well where they wanted within their range of transport, almost all of it public, and pocket. Angling was the perfect pastime.

Inexorably, fish life came under threat from the new chemical fertilizers, from the over-abstraction of water, spillage of sewage effluents; slurry (pig and cattle manure); and silage, which produces a deadly liquid that is more lethal than untreated sewage. All these harm fish and other water life when they are allowed to run off farmland into the nearest water-course. In many cases the authorities have been less than enthusiastic in pursuing polluters and the purity of the rivers has suffered in consequence. These horrors, plus the millions of enthusiastic anglers now pursuing their sport, mean that fishing is more difficult because there are fewer fish. But this is not an acceptance of defeat, far from it. Fishing tackle, new baits, and hugely improved techniques continue to develop, while many expert angler/authors have written books read by all anglers thirsty for knowledge about fishing and how to get the most from their sport.

Whales, of course, are not fishes although they share their environment. Many nations have hunted these mammals until many species are near extinction and even after world-wide legislation has agreed on the absolute necessity for conservation, some countries have continued to kill them, sometimes on the feeble pretext of 'scientific study'. The fecundity of fishes is far greater than man's ability to breed his own species, but it is still capable of being abused. Not so long ago the seas round the British Isles held such vast shoals of herring it was unimaginable that we could affect them. Unfortunately this is not so, for the trawlers of many nations congregated and harvested this fine food fish with such tenacity, and 'improved' fish-locating devices and techniques, that the herring's numbers are rapidly dwindling. Then com-

ABOVE One of the many
attractions of sea fishing is
the thrill of the size of the
catch, not to mention the
element of danger. Shark
fishing is no longer the blood
sport it once was: an expert
will remove the hook from the
mouth of this blue shark
before it is released
unharmed.

mercial fishers sought other species which they could harvest to near-extinction. These will be hunted and thinned to danger point, then others.

Despite the pessimism of the above, it should not be thought that as a sport angling has no future. Anglers have in large part spoken in one voice and enormous pressures are being put on the polluters and abstractors to clean up their rivers, and their act.

Coarse fishing is discussed under the appropriate heading in this book. The methods and tackles by which it is practised are peculiar to Europe; in the US, the fishing for the 'pan-fish' and species lower (in the anglers' estimation only) than the trout is called bait-fishing and a great deal of spinning is used. The concept of retaining the cyprinids after capture and then releasing them at the end of the session is not pursued across the Atlantic. Matchfishing for the coarse species, too, plays an important part in Britain and the Continent and many of the finer points of technique, tackle set-ups, and special baits are the result of top matchmen honing their methods in order to gain an advantage over the anglers on either side of them. Many of these advances in fishing technique are now employed in pleasure fishing.

A word about sea fishing. I have a particular regard for this facet of the sport, for me it is the best of all escapes. It is hugely rewarding to share a boat with no more than four close fishing friends and anchor out of sight of land over good fishing grounds, ie, an area of seabed holding sharp, rocky pinnacles which can rip and tear expensive commercial nets.

The fish species on these marks might be magnificent, hard-fighting pollack or cod, or handsome and solitary bass. At the foot of the rocks or in nearby wrecks may be mighty conger, strong as a horse. One of the thrills of sea fishing is the ever-present possibility of striking at an unseen fish and finding oneself attached to something twice as strong as you, something quite capable of pulling you over the side. Here is where the fishing rod comes into play, with its ability to absorb those first awesome plunges and pulls while the angler makes the necessary adjustments to the reel's braking system, enabling the conger to be fought to the surface.

Shark fishing can also be a source of sudden, frantic activity, and now that most shark anglers have realized the need for conservation, and bring the fish alongside to remove the hooks (only to be done by very experienced hands) and then release it, the sport has become honourable and not simply a bloody harvest.

So back to the beginning: what is fishing? A sport with many sides, which is open to all ages, both sexes and which has long ago broken any class barriers; a sport which respects the very surroundings in which it is practised, a way of life, a concern for all nature.

ABOVE During the summer months, holiday makers join seasoned anglers along Britain's coasts. The 'angling bug' is often caught at a young age.

COARSE FISHING

In the British Isles coarse fishing is now wholly a pleasure activity, a sport that can be practised by both sexes, young and old, the infirm and those blooming with health. It is a simple pastime enjoyed in most cases in green and pleasant surroundings and above all, in fresh air. This is one of the great attractions of angling, one can sit or stand and soak in the delights of the countryside. But open countryside is not a prerequisite for angling, there are rivers and canals running through built-up areas which often hold fish, and on Sunday mornings in sun, frost, rain, or snow, their towpaths can be lined with anglers quietly sitting, their attention riveted on that small orange float standing up at an angle from the water.

Never be fooled by that apparent inaction! The knowing angler might be sitting quietly, but if he is float-fishing his eyes are aware of every twitch or dip of the float. And he has to differentiate between the tiny, delicate nibble from a fish and the dip of a float as it is swirled about by wind or a passing fish. Even dragonflies alighting on a tiny quill float can make it dance and produce an instant reaction from the angler.

But why 'coarse'? The question has been posed a thousand times: is it a reflection of the difference between the past country-gentleman trout angler, for whom dry fly was the only fishing method, and the roach-seeking cloth-cap-and-muffler artisan? There was once a chasm between them; the worker never saw, let alone fished, the protected and bailiffed trout stream. The gentry were not all uncaring, but they were mostly quite ignorant of any other kind of fishing than the fly or trout. Even in some places today anything but trout and salmon are called vermin.

'Coarse' is now nothing more than an accepted title and not a description of the carp, roach, chub, and so on, and the pike and perch. And what other description would be so universally understood? It almost certainly reflects these species' poor eating qualities when the rivers teemed with those fish and diets had to be supplemented by pike. The flesh of the coarse species was described once as 'cotton wool stuffed with needles and tasting of mud'. I have eaten pike and found it not without merit, but unlike the tasty, oily sea fish, pike needs some culinary assistance to make it welcome to the palate.

Neither can the term coarse be considered as a description of the angler's tackle for roach and so on. Rods were once crude, or coarse. Branches of various woods, twigs, lengths of bamboo, all were put to use and to the end (before reels were invented) was tied string, twine, or silk, of which more later. No doubt the often-quoted bent pin on to which was impaled a worm or some luckless but handy insect, was used. Some of the old snap-tackles, gorges, trimmers and so on, lacked little finesse but they were designed to catch fish for the pot. They did just that. Today's pleasure coarse fisherman is a highly skilled sportsman using what we call 'high-tech gear'. His rod is made of man-made materials that are incredibly light; his reel is of carbon, his line an extended whisp of nylon. He has had the benefit of a wide-ranging literature written in most cases by able authors who knew their skill, and just as important, knew how to put it down in words. There is nothing coarse about the terminal tackle used to catch specimen roach.

There was a time when men fished the rivers and stillwaters for food, not for fun, although there was already an element of pleasure in the thrill of the chase. That thrill is still there today, but it is tempered with the knowledge that we just cannot keep on taking fish out of their element. The fecundity of fishes is greater, much greater than the human race, but it is still capable of being abused.

Consideration and care must be given to all species of fish. We no longer need to leave those deadly, circular trimmers out all night and then pull them in with the dead pike or perch hanging beneath them to provide a meal. The environment, too, is just as important. Many fish, the majority of species, will not thrive in polluted water, but except in a very small degree pollution is not something that can be laid at the feet of anglers. Industry and agriculture cause pollution and to our shame and that of our legislators, polluters are often allowed to continue their foul work in the interests of profit.

Coarse fishing in Britain has many unique sides to it. While American and some Continental people are quite happy to eat farm-bred common carp, and take home perch and pike after a day's fishing, the British coarse angler has had instilled into him the tenet that these and other 'coarse' species are sacrosanct, to be hooked, played to the net then released unharmed. As a conservation point, each species has its size limit below which the fish cannot be retained.

In this section of the book we are not concerned with the large number of sea fishes, the game fishes, the salmon, trouts, and other species that carry a still puzzling appendage just in front of the tail-fin, known as the adipose fin. It does not perform any swimming function, it has no bones, but it is one of the physical identification points in establishing whether a fish is 'coarse' or 'game'.

In the thirties, Frank Buck was a hunter-guide-cum-film-star in Africa who became known to film-goers. Hollywood saw the box-office appeal of making films in which heroic Frank sought lions, elephants and other suitably impressive wildlife 'for real' and captured them for various zoos. His films were called 'Bring 'em Back Alive' – but on the angler's heart should be engraved the words 'Put 'em *Back* Alive!' for unless he does that his thoughtlessness and the actions of the polluters will have destroyed the sport and pleasure of millions of anglers-to-be.

ABOVE Virtually weightless, but even so a dragonfly can produce just that tiny but misleading quiver that brings reaction from an alert angler.

OPPOSITE Trimmers are deadly, flat, circular wooden floats, coloured red one side, green the other. The dowel on the green side had the baited hook attached and floated that way up. When a fish took the bait it pulled the trimmer over so that the red side floated uppermost, signalling the capture.

WHERE CAN ONE FISH?

It is safe to say that above the reach of tidal movement (and to some extent even below it) all land and water, whether in a river or enclosed, belongs to somebody – some body is more accurate because legal bodies can own water as well as people – and therefore where there once was free access to some rivers there is now virtually none. So there are two things (fishing tackle apart) that the angler must be in possession of before he begins fishing: a permit from the owner to fish that water he wishes to fish, and a licence from the appropriate authority. These can be obtained in two ways, most fishing tackle shops will sell licences for periods of a day, a week, a month or a year for the waters in their area, and sometimes for waters outside that area.

The local tackle shop will also supply information about permits, and in many instances one can obtain them from bailiffs on the water. Bailiffs employed by authorities carry proper written warrant cards and have the powers of constables, so they can make life unpleasant for anglers fishing without a licence and permission. Fishing clubs which own or lease waters are wise to appoint their own bailiffs and in some cases every member of the club carries his membership card which describes him as a bailiff, although in this case his powers are limited.

WHEN CAN ONE FISH?

An Act of Parliament called the Salmon and Freshwater Fisheries Act 1923, consolidated in 1975, laid down what we now call the close season

for coarse fishes. It is from 15 March to 16 June inclusive 'or whatever period is substituted by byelaws' and in this period it is illegal to fish for the carps, the perch and pike and so on. The main consideration for the close season is that this is supposed to be the time when these fishes are spawning and so should be left undisturbed. Quite properly, this principle is without fault and laudatory – except that some cyprinids, the tench for one, have never read the Act and are known to extend their spawning season to late June, just when the coarse angler, his appetite whetted and sharpened by the enforced inaction of the close season is out in force and making up 'lost' fishing time with all the zest he can manage. But there the Act remains unchanged: no coarse fishing between 15 March and 16 June. There are some exceptions to the statutory close season and its powers cover England and Wales only, for Scotland's fishing is almost entirely confined to fishing for salmon and trout and their seasons vary from district to district. In other parts of Britain, there are some private, enclosed waters not part of any river system under the control of a Water Authority where coarse fishing is allowed the year round.

SPECIMEN HUNTING

It is probably safe to assume that every angler thinks of himself as a 'specimen hunter' if only for the reason that he hopes for a big fish every time his bait is taken. But for some anglers this yearning overcomes his ordinary civilized and decent fishing habits and turns him into a masochist disdaining everything but the dedicated search for THAT fish; the biggest, strongest, most notable specimen of whatever species has taken control of him. Facetious this may be, but specimen hunters form clubs to sit and talk about nothing but one species. Papers are written, books published all on one kind of fish.

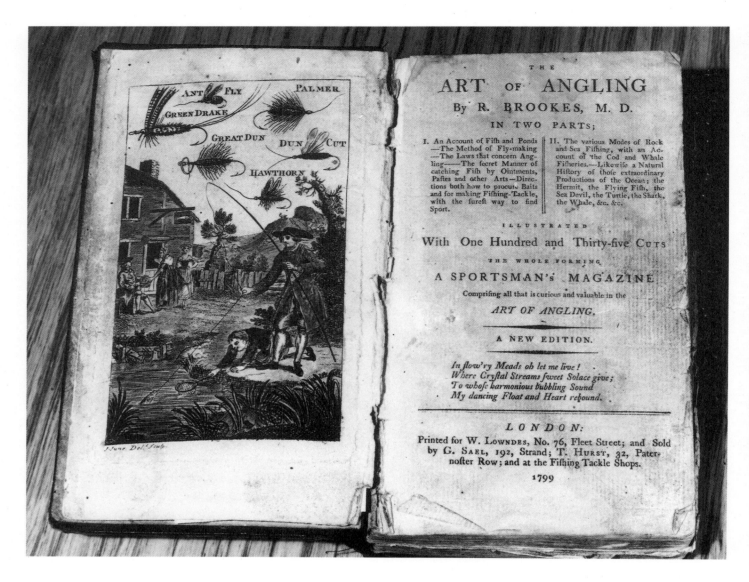

ABOVE Today's angling literature looks very different, but in many respects the advice of 200 years ago still holds. The tackle, however, is very different!

CLUBS AND SOCIETIES

The roving angler will often arrive at a water he has seen in passing or read about in the angling press. He is eager to test his skills on this water where particularly good fish have recently been caught. But when he gets there he sees a prominent notice which says:

PRIVATE FISHERY,
MEMBERS OF THE XXX
FISHING SOCIETY
ONLY

Our angler has travelled perhaps a long way only to find that he cannot fish the water. Sometimes he is lucky enough to see a water-bailiff who is empowered to sell him a day ticket for the water, so long as he has the appropriate licence, but more often than not the angler has to seek another water. The name and address of the Secretary of the private water will often be found on the notice-board and so an approach can be made for membership.

Any angler who wants to have access to waters without experiencing the annoyance of being prevented from fishing when he arrives would be recommended to join one of the large angling clubs, whose waters are open to members. Many fishing clubs are affiliated to federations whose collective waters can be available to members. Some famous societies control really first-class waters and hold inter-club matches for those interested in competitive fishing. But there are plenty of chances for pleasure fishing too.

Federations issue guide-books to the waters they control, with the dates of open competitions, local size limits, membership rules and so on. An additional advantage is that some of the larger clubs also have arrangements with their local tackle dealer who offers tackle at advantageous prices to members who produce their membership cards.

Belonging to an angling club can be nothing but an advantage. Younger members can listen to the collective experience of the old-timers and very often unwanted tackle is brought to club meetings for sale at knock-down prices for the benefit of other members.

All enclosed waters will deteriorate if left to do so. The surrounding vegetation will slowly encroach into the shallows, forming muddy areas where reeds grow. Then the reeds will give way to grasses and in a few years trees will be where there was once water. Sooner or later, and unless the water is topped up by a feeder-stream or spring, there will not be sufficient depth to support fish life.

This is where fishery management comes in. Federations and clubs which lease or own enclosed waters appoint experienced members who organize working parties in the close season. Depths are checked, swims renovated and platforms are renewed, fallen trees removed. Occasionally biologists are called in to check the fish stocks and advise on the introduction of species. This should never be done 'to see what happens' and is in fact illegal unless properly supervized.

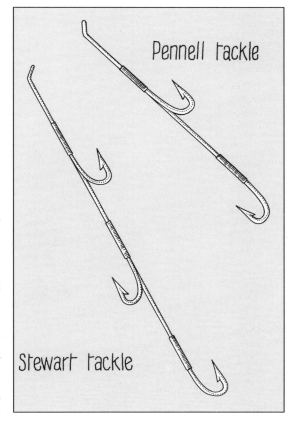

Pennell tackle

Stewart tackle

RODS

Early in the 19th Century, W B Daniel, in his classic *Rural Sports*, wrote that hazel was the wood generally used for rods, but cob-nut was longer and straighter. Then he added instructions about the prevention of wood-rot and the attacks from worms and beetles. Greenheart and willow, too, were considered very good. But it was not all that long before bamboo was found to be, at the time, the ideal substance. Then in the mid-19th Century it was found that if bamboo is carefully split into six sections and glued together it produces a rod with extraordinary strength and a 'life' in its movement which still today excites the traditionalist.

Man-made fibres now occupy the fore-front in fishing rods (and many other everyday items which were once of wood). First of all came rods in solid glassfibre, heralded as the latest thing, and naturally expensive. Then glassfibre strips were wrapped round a former and glued with a synthetic resin, the result being a rod with strength and lightness, after which the old solid-glass rods were shrugged off and described as 'liquorice sticks'. Today, boron and Kevlar, tomorrow – ? There is no doubt that the angler of today has at his disposal fishing rods that do not wear out, do not rot, do not break under any but the most extreme handling – or when they are trodden on, which is usually the fault of the angler who leaves them lying across a path.

Along the rod are affixed rings through which the line travels from the reel. There are good and bad rings, the best presenting the least resistance to the line when it is either wet or dry and which will not pull away

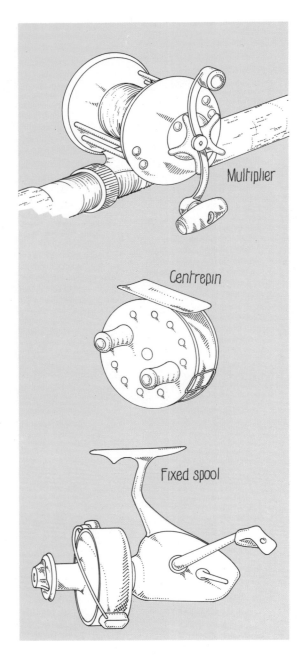

Multiplier

Centrepin

Fixed spool

from the rod while under tension. There are rods designed for specific kinds of fishing, from the really powerful carp rods capable of coping with 40lb (18kg) of wound-up *Cyprinus carpio* doing its utmost to swim into the nearest bank of thick weed, to the long, slender matchrod, which must have all the action in the tip to play and bring to the net the constant intake of small, and sometimes not-so-small shoal fish to amass a winning weight. Matchfishing will be discussed later in this section.

REELS

Reels to hold fishing line go back (like much else) to the Ancient Egyptians, but in Daniel's day the line was usually tied to the tip of the rod, which meant that the combined length of rod and line dictated the limit of the angler's fishing area. The Chinese had illustrated fishing reels 5000 years previously, but in Britain while reels, called winches, were introduced in the 18th Century, they did little but hold a reservoir of line, enabling the angler to cast further than previously.

Centre-pin reels, with the spools at right-angles to the rod, are still in use and are excellent when used in expert hands. Fairly long casts can be made, but distance is limited because it is difficult to control line being pulled off a free-running spool. Then in the 1920s Illingworth very nearly came up with the answer with his reel, on which the spool was rotated so that its axis was in line with the rod, allowing line to be pulled off by the weight of the terminal tackle with little friction. This is called the fixed-spool reel, and with refinements it is used by most coarse fishermen today. One problem was that of line spilling off the drum if it was over-filled, or snagging into what anglers call a 'bird's nest' and matting into a tangle that defies unravelling. The reel has a movable bale arm which allows line to be cast off the reel without friction. When the bale arm is engaged, the turning of the handle reels the line in and winds it on to the spool. Thus the modern fixed-spool reel, with closed face and skirted spool has revolutionized float fishing by making it easy to cast very light tackle to good distances.

There is another kind of centre-pin reel called a multiplier. Here, the spool is connected to a gear mechanism by which one turn of the handle produces two or three turns of the spool. This reel is ideal for spinning and fast retrieving.

LINES

Going back once more (and for the last time) to Daniel, this angler told his readers that 'the hair from a young, healthy, grey or white stallion, and which is of a pale transparent water colour, from the middle of the tail' was the best finishing line. There followed instructions for sorting, matching, leaving in clean spring water for 12 hours, drying, then sorting the hair into bundles of 'five or six score' to be tied at both ends. Lines of silk or hemp were also employed. But science came to the aid of the angler in the form of a man-made fibre we call nylon monofilament. This comes in breaking strains of 8oz (0.2kg) up to very strong lines used in deep-sea big-game sea fishing up to 100lb (45kg) b.s.

HOOKS

This most vital item in the angler's tackle box has its origins way back when flint, bone, fish spines, plant spines, were all used to catch fish, and some are used today in a few areas of the world. Today's machine-made hooks are strong and reliable and are manufactured in a wide variety of types designed for specific fishing purposes. The importance of

a hook is evident, for no matter how attractive the bait, how clever it has been cast to where fish are, how perfect (and expensive) the angler's rod, reel and line are, if the hook fails the fish is lost and all that expertise is to no avail.

Hooks are available tied to short lengths of nylon, but most anglers prefer to tie their own directly to the reel line. A special whipping knot is needed to tie spade-end hook, but a simpler knot fixed eyed hook to the line. For most species the coarse float-fisherman will use a single hook on the end of his line, but there are other kinds of hook with double or treble barbs, mostly used in plugs and spinners. The basic, modern hook is not the simple 'bent pin' but has a number of features, shown in the diagram. There are stainless steel hooks, which are fine but their sharpness is sometimes suspect. Most float-fishing hooks are of fine wire that has been tempered to give strength.

In selecting his hook the angler must check that it does not snap at the bend, check the point for sharpness and the barb that it is not cut too deep, which weakens its effectiveness and makes it liable to snap under pressure. The shank of a hook can be long or short, and selection depends upon the bait to be used. Maggots can be used in a hunch on a round-bend short-shank, while worms on the same hook just wriggle and writhe into an unattractive ball, so a long-shank, or two long-shanks in tandem, will hold the worm properly so that it will attract a roving fish. The gape varies with the model as does the bend and there are hooks with the point turned in or out.

Rust, too, has to be kept at bay, for there is nothing like it to eat into the metal so that the hook gives at the first slight pull. At the end of the session some anglers take their tackle down in a hurry and drop float, hook-link and hook into the tackle box and go home. If the hook and nylon is still wet rust will very quickly form and spread to other hooks. So carefully dry all the terminal tackle first, remove the hook and pop it into one of the small transparent envelopes that can be bought for this purpose. A square of folded newspaper will be as effective if the hook is dried first.

Hooks are the angler's prime link between him and the fish; they are important and must be chosen correctly for the proposed fishing method.

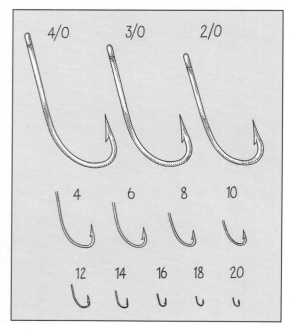

MATCHFISHING

There are many sportsmen for whom it is not enough to take part, to enjoy whatever they are doing for its own sake, they must compete. The runner who wants to come first, the thrower who must hurl the hammer or javelin furthest, the swimmer the fastest, the jumper the highest. The sport of angling is no different; there are millions of anglers who go to the waterside and fish happily with or without friends, in wonderful solitude, listening to the sounds of running water, or the songs of birds. Many in fact prefer the peace of the countryside; to have their small swim to themselves where they can fish quietly. As we have said before in these pages even the fish caught in such surroundings are a bonus.

But then there are the anglers who want to put their prowess against the other man, to catch more or bigger fish than him or her. The match-fishing scene today is a highly organized business followed keenly by the angling press, who well know the benefits of competition when it comes to selling their publications. The unknown matchman who finds a prime swim and who has the ability to fish it properly will have his name and fame spread far and wide, especially if he has toppled a big-name, an angler tipped to win the event.

ABOVE Matchfishing is a specialised form of fishing and those who pit their skills against other anglers become highly efficient at their craft of finding, holding and catching more fish than the rest of the field.

It has been said that the reason for the greater percentage of match-fishing being done in the industrial areas of England is because this is the only way to get access to the prime fishing waters. Perhaps so, but the rivers and canals in these areas are not waters that hold large fish. The Industrial Revolution, and more recently the effect of agricultural chemicals posed a threat which was hardly recognized as being so when the rivers were full of fish.

Matchfishing, then, is about competitive fishing. There once used to be a National Angling Championship fished on one day, when the cream of the matchfishing fraternity met and challenged each other. The long stretch of river was divided into 'pegs' and each one numbered. Then the matchmen came along and drew lots for the pegs, those picking swims likely to produce the winning weight were happy, those finding that their swim was unlikely to do much were resigned but determined to fish as hard as they could.

The great, late Billy Lane, winner of many contests, would trundle his wheelbarrow of groundbait along the bank, settle into his position and keep his tackle out of the water until the maroon boomed out to signal the start. Billy would then proceed to hurl fist-sized balls of groundbait like hand-grenades out into the selected spot until one felt that the river-level must surely rise, and his baited hook would plop over that underwater mound. But the carpet of breadcrumbs, bran, meal and all kinds of 'secret' additions, plus some samples of hookbait, would attract then hold the bream shoals which were the matchman's target, and the bream would soon begin to come to the net. At the end of the allotted time out would come the bulging keepnet and the weigh-in would begin under careful scrutiny. Another attraction was the village of bookmakers who shouted the odds and who knew a good deal about probable winning swims and who had picked their peg numbers.

Now there is a series of eliminators. Leagues and points and much of the romance has gone out of the Championship and the 'sudden death' atmosphere, and refinements in tackles and methods have overtaken the once 'sure way' to win. Yesterday's kings of the match world would not occupy their thrones today. It is the age of the swimfeeder, bait-dropper, springtip, quivertip, and target-board. The fact that the large bream shoals are no longer so abundant, means fish are harder to find. These things have changed the matchfishing scene. The matchman of today is a highly skilled operator and he has to be when the fish are fewer. He has 36ft-long (12.1m) carbon poles and float-rods of the same material, all of which weigh ounces, specialist pole floats, wagglers, stick-floats and above all the experience of fishing difficult waters in order to create winning totals.

Open matches are held every weekend and the angling press runs lists of matches where the angler can turn up, pay his entry fee of between a few pounds and £10 (up to $6), and try his hand against allcomers. The prizes vary according to numbers of entries and cost of tickets, but it is not unusual for the winner to take home a few hundred pounds.

Matchfishing is not every angler's delight, but for those who need the thrill of competition it is an exciting and challenging part of the sport. Fame (in angling circles) and some fortune await the successful fisherman who can learn the watercraft, the skills, the habits of fish, the mysteries of baits and mixing groundbaits, then spend long days in wind, snow, rain, and heat finding the right combinations. The apprenticeship is long and hard and one question remains: when one enters a contest to win, does any of the pleasure of solo angling remain? I hope so.

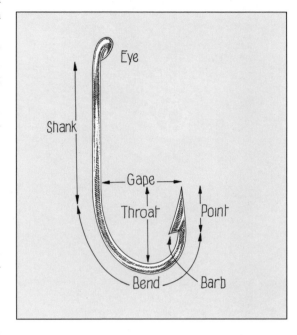

The Coarse Species

ABOVE Len Cacutt found this fossil fish acting as a door-stop in a Dorset village. From such clues we know much about the evolution of the huge number of fish species.

The species of fish that coarse anglers catch are divided into two main categories, the carp-type species and the predators. These will be the indigenous fishes, found in our rivers and enclosed waters since the ending of the last Ice Age and the formation of the North Sea and English Channel. Previous to that, large rivers of the Continent flowed across the North Sea and it is from them that our coarse species emanate. Fish species introduced artificially by man will be described later in the appropriate chapter.

The carp-types (known in the United States rather unfortunately as minnows) are the most numerous, ranging from the impressive carp itself, the crucian carp, two breams, roach, rudd, chub, tench, dace, barbel, minnow, gudgeon and their weights run from carp of 44lb (20kg) down to minnows and gudgeon of an ounce or two. The barbel and dace apart, all these fish can be found in both running and still waters. They are by and large shoaling fish, moving in numbers usually in well-established areas where they have been conditioned to find food – small invertebrates, water-living insects, terrestrial insects that have been blown on to the water surface, berries and fruit fallen from vegetation overhanging the water. This family of fishes is the largest in the world and has some 2,000 species. On the continent of Europe the carp family has a large number of related cyprinid species but these do not come within the scope of this volume.

CARP

The prime carp species is the common carp, *Cyprinus carpio*. Taxonomists, those scientists who list and classify animals with Latin generic and specific names in order that people speaking different languages will know which fish is being referred to, describe only one carp (ignoring the crucian carp which *is* a different species). However there are domesticated varieties of this fish; a large, barrel-shaped one and a longer 'wildie'. All carp have descended from introductions hundreds of years ago, some say back in Roman times. There are also carp with a few large scales near the lateral line, those fish known as mirror carp. Then there are scaleless, naked or leather carp. The pursuit of very large carp has become hugely important for many anglers. The late Richard Walker, a highly intelligent and innovative angler, stalked and finally hooked a massive 44lb (20kg) carp from a private pool in Herefordshire. The fish was easily the heaviest member of its species caught in Britain and was accorded the honour of being given residence in the Aquarium at London Zoo until it died of old age.

ABOVE A carp isn't glamorous but it fights with bulldog tenacity and great strength.

CRUCIAN CARP

The beloved crucian is a small cousin of the mighty and powerful common carp and is found where many of its relatives would not survive. Any farm pond, thick with weed and overgrown, might well have its crucian population to provide great sport for young anglers.

BREAM

There are two breams, the silver and the common or bronze bream. Both
are slab-sided, deep-bodied fish of winter and summer, but the silver
bream is a separate species and now rare in Britain even in the Eastern
counties. It is not unknown for anglers inexperienced in fish identification
to claim a 'record' silver bream when in fact they had hooked a small
common bream. This fish often forms the main weight of a match
fisherman's bag.

BARBEL

For power and dogged resistance to being reeled in there is little to beat a
double-figure barbel, a fish which stays down on the clean, gravelly
bottom of fast, pure streams, where it lies between banks of streamer
weed, waiting for food morsels to trundle downstream towards it. Barbel
can grow to considerable sizes and this allied to their considerable
strength makes any large specimen a doughty fighter and one very difficult to get to the waiting net.

CHUB

Then there is the chub, a large-mouthed, powerful resident of clear rivers and often found in the company of brown trout, where the water bailiffs take great trouble to eradicate the 'nuisance' chub and pike. This gives rise to very welcome visits in the close trout season by in-the-know anglers to waters usually reserved for and by game fishermen. The object of the exercise is to remove coarse species. This is one coarse fish that will eat anything edible. Its large mouth can accommodate fish of all species, crayfish, molluscs, insects and water-plants which enables the angler to bait with the widest range of offerings. I have taken chub on plugs, worms and maggots as well as many other baits.

DACE

Like the chub, another fish inhabits the fast, gravel-bedded streams and mixes with the trout. This fish is the dace and its old title 'dart' says all that can be said about its movements. The dace dashes here and there just below the surface, its silver flanks glittering as it turns and twists.

ABOVE There is no fishing style or bait which will not catch a chub, from float-fishing with maggot and fish-bait to spinner and plug.

ABOVE A surface-
feeder, the rudd will take an
artificial offered on fly tackle.

RUDD

As a sought-after fish the rudd regularly pops in and out of the angling limelight. The trouble is that unlike the roach (which it resembles superficially) the rudd has much more of a local distribution. Where it is found, and where an enclosed water holds few if any predators, the rudd also has a habit of undergoing population explosions. This results in large numbers of adult but stunted fish. These then exhaust the available food supply, when the population drops until the cycle starts again. Again unlike the roach, rudd tend to take their food either just below the surface or on it. This gives the coarse angler his chance to try out the fly rod, and many a dedicated trout fisherman started his liking for fly fishing by this means.

GRAYLING

This species shares waters and breeding seasons with the coarse fishes and so is considered as such. Handsome and very active, the grayling makes excellent eating because of its game lineage, but the angler must be sure that it is sizable before taking it home for the table. While the grayling is officially a 'coarse' fish it has close links with the salmonids. For instance it has the adipose fin and this is where the beautiful creature breaks the rules – for here we have a 'game' fish with 'coarse' habits; it joins the coarse fishes in their spawning time, the spring. In fact it seems to like the company of chub and dace and this led to the grayling being regarded as a coarse fish. A great friend, Harvey Torbett, made what is for me the ultimate description of this very beautiful creature: 'Nothing will teach the grayling its manners and the responsibility of the adipose fin.'

ABOVE Grayling from a stream in Derbyshire, England. Though these fell to bait, they readily take a fly.

ABOVE A specimen roach
which weighed 2lb 1oz (1kg)
when captured. Note the red
eye, from which the species
got its old name.

ROACH

No doubt, the roach, (old-time anglers called it 'Red-eye'), is traditionally the coarse angler's main target. A handsome fish, it is found in rivers and stillwater and grows to respectable sizes up to 4lb (1.8kg). It can be taken on most baits that are offered but at the same time is wary. One attraction is that it is both a summer and winter fish.

TENCH

The coarse fishing season, which opens on 16 June every year, sees anglers out at the crack of dawn fishing for tench. The fisherman artist/ author Bernard Venables described it as 'that fat, happy beauty'. This handsome, chunky golden fish, once thought to have medicinal properties and therefore 'excused' eating by hungry pike, is a summer species and goes with quiet pools, lily-pads and roving dragonflies. The species is unusual in that it displays sexual dimorphism, a physical difference between the species. In the case of the tench there is a skeletal difference which affects the shape of the pelvic fins.

ABOVE An impressive catch of tench, quite the most handsome of the cyprinids. They will be returned unharmed immediately after being photographed.

ABOVE Welsh anglers
talk of their salmon and trout,
but this beautifully marked
26lb (12kg) pike came from a
water in Wales.

PIKE

The main British predators of fish (man apart!) are the pike and perch.
There is a huge store of highly entertaining (but unreliable) folk-tales
about the pike's ability, even liking, for ducklings, other water-fowl and
even small dogs, while in not-so-recent times there have been the Victorian equivalent of tabloid newspapers carrying shock-horror stories of
paddlers having their ankles seized by 'angry' pike! But to return to
reality, pike will take quite sizable fish, as the Vincent brothers of two
decades ago knew. They fished the Norfolk Broads for pike and used 5lb
(2.2kg) fish of their own species as livebait! That the pike can reach very
heavy weights was proven by 'pikeologist' Fred Buller, who in his important book 'The Domesday Book of Mammoth Pike' listed 270 of them over
35lb (15.8kg).

PERCH

The perch belongs to the vast family of Perciformes, fishes with spined fins, which has a large number of salt-water members. This fish has an intriguing reputation. As a small, pugnacious, prettily striped fish it can be caught easily by small boys fishing with the crudest fishing tackle and little or no fishing guile. No doubt that the sight of this handsome fish, reeled in by the jubilant youngster, in many cases would set him or her on a lifetime's love of angling. But when it reaches weights of 4lb (1.8kg) and over it is a different fish. Reaching weights of 4½lb (2kg) or more, it is powerful and cunning and is not so easily tempted to take the proffered worm.

BLEAK, GUDGEON AND MINNOW

These are three small cyprinids that can populate a water in very large shoals. To the angler seeking larger fish they have a nuisance value well beyond their size, worrying and plucking at baits far too big for their mouths. These fish serve as food for chub, perch and pike and also provide attractive deadbaits for pike and perch.

ABOVE A hungry perch will throw itself at any bait. Spinning is the traditional method for them, but this one fell to a worm trotted downstream beneath a float.

LEFT The tench is a favourite coarse species which has anglers up at dawn at the start of the coarse fishing season.

RIGHT AND OPPOSITE Two species of carp. The mirror carp (right) is recognized by the large scales near the lateral line. The prime species (opposite) is of course, the common carp.

BELOW This beautiful 10.6lb (4.8kg) rainbow trout was caught at Newhouse Reservoir, Devon.

Methods of Coarse Fishing

FLOAT FISHING

The easiest way to practise coarse fishing (and one or two kinds of sea fishing) is by the use of a float. But before setting out to obtain floats, take advice from one who has fallen into the trap – do not go into a fishing tackle shop and choose floats by starting at one end of the row of float boxes and working your way along, selecting numbers of those attractive, 'fishy-looking' models in bright reds, oranges and greens. You will certainly come home with a colourful, impressive collection but you might as well put them straight into your display cabinet, because ten-to-one experience will reveal that only two or three will 'catch' fish for you, and your confidence in them will tend to make you ignore the others.

A float's job is to indicate to the angler that there is action in the area of the baited hook. It is not always from a fish that is taking the bait, for sudden movements – flapping fins or nudges of the line – can make the float twitch, gyrate, bob and wobble. In time experience will enable you to spot the false 'bite' from the real thing. Today, float-fishing has developed very nearly into an art-form, with many kinds of float available. Some of these are more attractive to anglers in the tackle shops than they are effective as sensitive supporters of a baited hook.

At one time, most floats were quills from birds' flight feathers. They ranged in size from quite large ones from swans, peacocks and geese to slender crow quills, which are still regarded by many anglers as the ultimate in fine, sensitive float-fishing. The long, sharp quills from porcupines are also well known as providing good floats. The porcupine is not a bird but one angling writer forgot this and suggested to his readership that they 'strip the feathers' from the animal's quills before turning them into floats.

Float shapes and actions are many and varied, but those used by the beginner are the quills: the balsa-bodied Avon, which comes in a number of sizes to accommodate different weights and has the line running through small rubber bands at top and bottom; the waggler, which has an antenna top and supports the line on the bottom-end only; and stick-floats which are weighted so that only the tip projects above the surface. While it can be difficult to see at times, this helps float fishing in a wind because there is so little to create resistance. There are also sliding floats, which come into their own when very deep water is being fished. The slider can be set on the line, with a stop knot positioned to fish the hookbait at the required depth.

What is known as the 'pressure of fishing', the effect on fish of the continual presence of anglers and baited hooks, and a natural caution of man, bred of being hooked and released, has in many waters tended to keep the fish well away from the banks. To catch them, fine tackle must be cast well out and in part the problem can be solved by the use of a bubble float. This is a transparent plastic sphere which can be filled or partly filled with water and provides an adequate weight when long-distance casting is necessary.

Since no other float is used for bite indication, the bubble-float does the job. With a bite there is no dip or bob, the bubble-float usually slides away or drops below the surface if the fish is big. An advantage of this float is that it has the natural appearance of a bubble on the surface and is not so likely to scare fish as the obvious shape of the float.

Beneath the float hangs the line, to which is added the baited hook. In order to suspend the bait, weight is needed to cock the float so that the

ABOVE For small livebait the float must be buoyant enough to support it but not so clumsy that the take is masked. The bait is being worked between banks of streamer weed.

line hangs properly and in just enough tension to register a bite when a fish takes. The tension is supplied by weight which up to a couple of years ago was in the form of lead split-shot, which came in a range of sizes from tiny 'dust' shot to 'swan' shot of which a few would weigh an ounce.

Then came reports of swans found dying of lead poisoning and it was not long before the blame was placed at the feet (or rather, the lead shot) of anglers, whose lost or discarded lead shots, it was claimed, were ingested by swans. Nothing was said about the vast quantities of lead shot fired from 12-bore shotguns whose owners were aiming at waterfowl. So there appeared the Control of Pollution (Anglers' Lead Weights) Regulations 1986. This Act prohibited the importation and use of lead, including lead in compound or alloy, for the purpose of weighting fishing lines below 0.06 grams or more than 1oz (28.36g). The tackle manufacturing trade had to come up with something quickly which of course it soon did and a range of lead substitutes is now available, some of which do the job once done by ordinary lead quite well.

The float-fishing rod will be between 10–12ft (3–3.6m) long and have an action known as 'all through', in other words the whole of the rod reacts to a fighting fish and not just the tip section. Before the universal use of glassfibre and carbon for rod materials, test curves were used to describe the rod's capability in terms of the maximum line breaking strain for the rod. The test curve was the pull in pounds needed to bend to the horizontal the tip of a vertically held rod. The test curve was multiplied by 5, so that if 1lb 8oz (0.6kg) was arrived at, this is multiplied by 5, giving 7lb 8oz (3.4kg). Thus the maximum line b.s. for a rod with a test curve of 1lb 8oz was 7lb 8oz. However, with the vastly improved strength of the man-made materials of today's rods the test curve concept is going out of fashion.

ABOVE Two forms of bubble-float, which can be used when an adverse wind is blowing to make float-fishing difficult.

OPPOSITE There are many kinds of bite-indicator, some electronic and complex, others simple. This orange-coloured ball is clearly visible against the green and blue background of grass and water.

The reel will be a fixed-spool loaded with nylon of about 1lb (445g) breaking strain (usually just printed as 'b.s.') Float fishing is the kind most practised, but the beginner should avoid a habit easily acquired — that of sticking to one kind of tackle after finding that it catches fish. Whatever the conditions of water and weather, one's tackle must be set up to cope. When some anglers, having sat for hours without a bite, say that the fish are 'off' it is likely that they have not changed either their float, hook length, bait, fishing depth or their weight pattern; they have not tried to find out which style was needed on the occasion.

Casting a float-fishing rig is usually done by the under-arm method, with the tackle swung out so that the weight precedes the float. The fixed-spool reel allows casts of a considerable distance with this kind of tackle.

Unless there is a side wind, float-fishing in stillwater means that the float will stay cocked in one place, with the bait positioned to be found by feeding fish. In running water the float can also be held back, but a style known as trotting the stream allows the float to move downstream with the current, held back so that the baited hook precedes it. This method takes the bait along at just the right speed to attract fish.

Bite detection mostly involves watching for the float either to dip quickly or slide away as a fish takes the bait. But if the float is attached at the bottom only and most of the weight just over-depth the float will be held very low in the water. When a fish takes the bait and lifts it from the bottom the weight is taken off, with the result that the float pops up, and the angler strikes. There are a number of refinements to float fishing which can be practised once the basic skills are acquired.

LEGERING

The other basic method in fishing is legering (often seen spelled as 'ledgering'). The term probably derives from the French *leger*, which means 'light' or 'buoyant'; *leger* also refers to being dexterous, which could well have some connection with legering, ie not using a float but holding the bait on the bottom by means of a weight which is just enough to hold without creating resistance for a taking fish.

Weights over 1oz (28.35 grams) were not affected by the legislation banning the use of lead shot and these come in shapes which are dictated by the manner in which they operate. Leger weights are described as 'coffins', 'bombs', 'barrels' or 'bullets' and their shapes show how they are intended to cope with varying kinds of river or lake beds. The flat coffin is drilled through lengthwise so that the line runs through it. The squared edges of this lead sits on the bottom and resists the pull of the current, holding the baited hook where the angler feels it is best placed. The bomb, known originally as the Arlesey Bomb, was just one of the late Richard Walker's great angling achievements and it has an in-built swivel at the fine end and is used where the water is deep. The barrel lead, with the line running through it, will be rolled by the current in an arc across the riverbed; the bullet does the same but allows the angler to move the baited hook over a wider area. All leger weights come in a variety of sizes over 1oz (28.35 grams).

When necessary, longer casts are possible when legering. The rig is either swung out under-hand or with a side cast and correct use of the thumb on the line as it is pulled off the fixed-spool reel gives control. It is important that a taking fish does not feel the resistance of the weight, so the leger tackle settles on the bottom with the reel line usually running through an eye of the swivel on the weight. Another leger rig is the

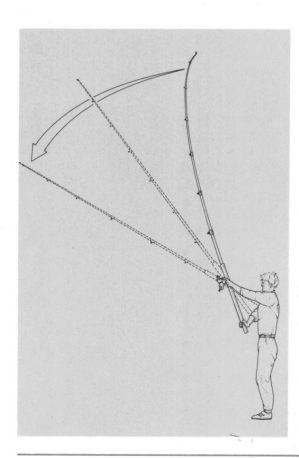

paternoster. Here the weight lies on the bottom and the hook-link holds the baited hook at a level at which the angler estimated the fish to be feeding.

Without a float to indicate a bite, the leger-fisherman must rely on some other visual or tactile signal. The basic method is to rest a fingertip on the line just away from where it leaves the reel spool. With experience the angler can detect the difference between wind or current tugging on the bowed line and the attentions of a taking fish. If the rod is held high, the tiniest quiver of the rod tip will be reacted to by a strike. Sometimes there is no possibility of doubt, when a sizable fish sucks in the bait and dashes away, bringing the rod-tip down smartly. Bite detectors will be discussed in the section on fishing accessories. Some legering techniques have the rod at right-angles to the water and the addition of a swing or spring-tip, an accessory which is screwed into a ready-made aperture in the rod-tip, gives very definite bite indications. A refinement to this technique is the erection of a target-board in front of the rod tip, usually chequered or marked in coloured zones. When the swing or quiver-tip flutters or dips its movement is starkly shown against the target-board instead of the grass or mud background.

FLOAT-LEGERING

The two main coarse fishing styles can be combined by using a float and sufficient weight to hold the bait on the bottom. With the baited hook on the bottom, and the line running up to the float set at an angle and kept taut, the sensitivity of this rig is acute, responding to the smallest bites.

SPINNING

The use of lures is as old as fishing itself, although the method of casting spinners and plugs today has resulted from the emergence of the centre-pin and multiplier reels. Without these aids, spinning is far more difficult, as anyone who has tried to cast a light-weight spinner with a centre-pin will attest.

There is a single, basic difference between a plug and a spinner. The plug, which can be single or jointed, is cast out and retrieved, in the process acting like a fish by swimming erratically, or diving and rising. Vanes on the plug can be adjusted to produce deep or shallow dives. Spinners depend on their attractiveness by embodying a revolving element which as the spinner is retrieved flashes and sparkles like the scales of a small fodder-fish.

Rods for spinning are different from those used in float or leger fishing. Spinning lures or plugs vary in weight and distances are going to vary too, so the rod must match the weight of the lure and how far the angler feels he must cast. There are streams where distance is not important but the accuracy of the cast is. I remember using a spinner while fishing the River Chess near Uxbridge. It is not a wide river but has gravelly shallows and banks of streamer weed. The fish were lying in those banks of weed and so my small spinner had to be plopped gently at the head of the weed and worked down between the runs. The distance to be cast was no more than 10 yards, but accuracy was needed.

On a large enclosed water, where the pike might be lying along the edge of reeds but where the angler cannot get to without creating a great deal of disturbance, he may have to cast from a shore or boat 30 yards away. The rod needed must be able to do with a heavy plug, quite unlike that for the Chess.

ABOVE With a rather garish hat as a size indication, a selection of treble-hooked plugs. The hat is not recommended.

OPPOSITE The target-board in action. The slightest movement of the rod tip is instantly seen against the radiating lines on the white board.

Another form of spinning uses a lure called a spoon, which has a blade that often wobbles instead of spinning. Again it is the motion of the lure, the flash, and the vibrations transmitted through the water that attract the fish.

PLAYING A FISH

After striking and finding that a fish is hooked, the angler must then take steps to bring it close. Little fish usually need nothing more than reeling in, but there will come a time when a strike is followed by a powerful tug and line starts to be pulled off the reel. This is where skill comes in, for the fish must be played until its strength is sapped and it can be drawn close. Never wind the handle of a fixed-spool reel while line is being pulled off, all you will do is weaken the line and put twists into it.

The rod must be held at the correct angle so that its springiness and length acts to sap the fish's power, and this is wherer the proper balance between rod and line b.s. comes in. The angler must know the strength of the line and be able to judge how much tension he can apply without the line breaking. As the fish moves to left or right, so the rod must be angled to apply side-strain on the fish. Continual pressure by the rod on the fish will eventually weaken it sufficiently to be drawn close. A deep-fighting fish has to be 'pumped', that is the rod is held high and the handle wound, not to pull the fish up, but to wind the rod down towards the water surface. When it is there, stop winding the handle and try to raise the rod, and the fish. If the fish is till too strong, play it until it can be pumped up until it lies on the surface.

WHAT TO DO WITH THE FISH – THE LANDING-NET

When a fish has been hooked and brought close to the angler, it might be small enough to be lifted from the water, unhooked and released. But if a big and strong fish is hooked on light line and tackle any attempt to lift it from the water will probably result in broken line and a lost fish with the hook still in its mouth and a length of nylon trailing behind. This is not bad luck, it is bad fishing. Of course, one cannot stop a big fish from taking a single maggot on a small hook, fished on 1lb (0.45kg) b.s. line. Landing-nets are described in the chapter on accessories.

This is where the landing net becomes necessary. Never bring the fish close, then try to scoop the fish out with the net. Well before the fish is near, have the net itself below the surface and then draw the fish over it. Not until it is safely in should the angler lift the handle of the net and swing it inshore.

Coarse fishing waters

All freshwaters in the British Isles have been moulded by the retreat 10,000 years ago of the Ice Age glaciers. Even in the south of England which was not covered by ice the huge run-offs and warming of tundra, the formation of the North Sea and English Channel were all instrumental in creating new rivers and changing the direction of others.

In any form of angling, where he or she fishes depends on where the fish are. This kind of knowledge can be learned from experience (by far the best method) or obtained from other anglers or in tackle shops. In coarse angling there is a very wide range of water types, from fast-flowing streams to mature, meandering rivers, from small farm ponds to man-made reservoirs. The species themselves need certain conditions for

ABOVE Parks, even in the heart of London, offer some good fishing. This angler in Battersea Park, under the shadow of the shell of the great Power Station, is netting a very sizable fish.

OPPOSITE Weirs can provide fascinating and rewarding fishing. Just below the lips the water is full of oxygen and food particles are swept round. Fish will dart into the disturbed water to take them. The hat is familiar!

them to exist and breed and so each kind of water will hold one or more fish species, with some overlap where a fish such as a chub can live in fast gravel-bedded streams as well as slow, muddy-bottomed rivers. From their source, which may be a small spring or the run-off from perpetual snow high up on mountains, rivers flow towards either the sea or to a meeting, known as a confluence, with another water-course.

FAST HIGHLAND WATERS

These usually begin where the water gains momentum down the steep slopes and the only fish present will be small but adult brown trout, stone-loaches, miller's thumb and minnows. A little farther down the grayling will begin to be found in company with the trout and the smaller species which form part of their food chain. These waters are cold, have a high oxygen content and run between rocky ledges, round boulders, and over stones and gravel. The weed growth found in highland and moorland waters is thin and sparse, which means there is only a small population of the insect life upon which many fish feed. In these areas, too, are found mountain lakes, many of them residual waters from the retreat of the Ice Age glaciers of 10,000 years ago. Some of these deep, ancient lakes hold species of fish that were once migratory but whose populations were cut off as the land rose, due to the weight of perhaps a mile of ice being removed as the Ice Age glaciers melted.

SLOWER WATERS

As the terrain loses its steepness the speed of the river slows, allowing more species to live there; fish which can cope with the lessening push of the water. Here, barbel, chub and dace are found, the brown trout and grayling are still present, with the smaller fodder fish such as minnows, bull head and gudgeon. The oxygen content is still high here, but with a slower current the depth can be greater and when the weather is warm there may be a lessening of oxygen in the deepest pools.

MATURE RIVERS

This area sees the wide, stately flowing rivers running through the rich pasture land of the plains, meandering in beautiful loops which slowly join to leave isolated those picturesque ox-bow lakes. The weed growth is lush and abundant and holds many kinds of aquatic insect life upon which the fish feed. Here are bream, roach, rudd, carp, tench and their predators the pike and perch – and still the trout. Here, too, are enclosed waters, some natural, some man-made. All that are capable of doing so will hold fish because if they are not introduced by man, birds will pick fish ova up on their feet and transport them to other waters where they will hatch if the conditions are right. In some Bedfordshire lakes the wels is found after having been released there many years ago.

Where man has river-craft he needs moorings for them and bridges of all kinds cross the rivers. These places are the favourite haunts of fish, they give shelter when the summer sun reaches down below the surface; they create weedy areas where insect life provides food; they create eddies where food particles are swirled round and round to be picked up by the fish; in short, they provide the perfect living environment for fish. The angler has found that these places are prime fishing spots and has worked out the best ways to fish them.

OPPOSITE Romney Marsh does not always look as inviting as this, but it is typical of fen and drain country.

ABOVE Freshwater mussels make excellent baits for many coarse species. They are found in profusion in the silt and mud bottoms of slow rivers or enclosed waters.

OPPOSITE Coarse fishing at Bollingey Lake in Cornwall.

LEFT A fisherman uses a fixed spool reel at Shillamill, Lanreath, Cornwall.

RIGHT Many reservoirs offer good stillwater trout fishing, as at Newhouse Reservoir, Devon.

BELOW Plant life can aid the angler; at Shillamill the rushes along the waters edge harbour many of the insects which attract fish.

Many places on waters are known to anglers as 'hot-spots', where fish are known to be found regularly. They might be where the patrolling paths of fish meet, for fish do have fixed movements; springs welling up will oxygenate the water and again fish will tend to congregate there, as will the knowing anglers.

THE FENS, CANALS, DRAINS

When the Industrial Revolution gave rise to canals, joined to the sea and the river, fish such as roach and bream quickly occupied these new waters. Many of these canals have now fallen into disuse and vegetation is encroaching from the banks, but groups of interested parties are beginning to revive these waters so that they can provide the fishing that once thrived there. In East Anglia, the Fens, that maze of narrow drainage systems, and the Broads, man-made in medieval times, provide an ideal environment for many fish species, although the holiday boat traffic has lessened the quality of the waters in this area. The Fenland drains were the original home of the introduced zander, but this predator has found its way into many more areas. It was feared that the zander would compete for food with pike but this has not happened.

WEIRS AND SLUICES

In places along a water-course there will be weirs or sluices where at times water is needed to be held back so that some control can be exercised over the flow. The flow of water over the weir apron will create hollows where the highly oxygenated water swirls in eddies which hold all kinds of food particles. Here, fast-water species such as dace and chub provide really enjoyable fishing.

LAKES AND PONDS

There are a number of words to describe naturally formed enclosed water: meres, tarns, lochs, loughs, and they depend mostly on where these are located. From the largest lake to the smallest farm pond, fish will usually be found unless the water has been polluted and all life in it killed. Many large waters hold a variety of coarse (and often game) fish, but the smallest pond can also carry swarms of adult but stunted fish, such as rudd, which are ideal for young anglers to begin to learn their fishing skills. The lakes and ponds of Britain's towns and commons often hold quite sizable fish, and the photograph of an angler fishing the lake in Battersea Park is illustration of just one kind of water.

THE ESTUARY

As the river nears the sea it broadens and perhaps becomes shallower. In its tidal reaches, where the water is brackish and the river level rises and falls with the tides, a few freshwater fish, the pike for one, will occupy the same waters as the flounder and the mullets. Here, too, sea trout and salmon will be found in the appropriate time of year on their way upstream to spawn. In a few rivers the shads run up at certain seasons.

ABOVE These maggots are just beginning to turn into casters. The maggots dyed pink and yellow are no longer available.

Coarse Fishing Baits

It is usual to begin a description of coarse fishing baits with the maggot, the universal attractor which has probably accounted for every fish species found in freshwater — and a few which live in brackish water and even saltwater. Even pike have been caught on a small hook baited with a bunch of maggots intended for roach or tench.

MAGGOTS

Shop-bought maggots for fishing purposes, also known as gentles, are the grubs or larvae of the housefly, greenbottle and bluebottle, which all belong to the insect family Odonata. They can be bred without difficulty at home but unless there is a very long garden which is not surrounded by other habitation, domestic and local pressures prevail to convince the would-be maggot breeder to desist. One reason is that the process gives rise to unpleasant odours. Even the highly organized, properly set-up commercial maggot-breeder has a hard time with local authorities who react when smells from the breeding sheds reach nearby houses.

The process is not difficult. The basic element is a food source for the maggot and this can be chicken or meat. When put in a container such as a biscuit tin and left in the open, flies will be attracted to the food source and lay their eggs on it, which can be seen in tiny white clusters. The meat is then wrapped in paper and after a few days the eggs hatch and the small maggots begin feeding on the meat.

A few more days and the maggots will have grown to half-an-inch or so and stop feeding. They are then placed in bran for two days, sieved and stored until needed. Maggots have a sweet tooth, so if some brown sugar is given them they fatten well. The natural process is for maggots to feed, then turn into brown, hard-skinned chrysalids. This stage lasts a few days before the adult fly emerges to start the breeding cycle all over again. In warm weather all the processes are quickened, but if they are put in a secure container and placed in the domestic fridge their actions will slow and the maggots will lie still.

However, maggot breeding is best left to the professional, who produces them in millions for every weekend's fishing. The ordinary housefly is responsible for a small maggot known as a 'squatts' which are thrown in to attract fish. The bluebottle produces larger maggots which 'sit' better on the small hooks used with this bait. When one species of bluebottle lays eggs on the heart of a pig or sheep the resulting very soft, white maggots are known as 'gozzers'. The fly called the greenbottle also gives rise to small maggots which for some reason are known as 'pinkies' (not the 'pinkies' of American terminology).

It was once considered good fishing tactics to colour white maggots by putting them in dyes. Auramine O would give yellow maggots, Chrysio-dine B gave them an orange appearance, and Rhodamine B made them red. The different colours, it was suggested, attracted fish at various times. Sadly, the dyes were alleged to have a carcinogenic effect on those who handled them, so the practice was quickly dropped and dealers stopped offering them for sale.

When hooking maggots it is very important to do so without effecting the wriggle which is so attractive to fish. This is achieved by using very small, thin-wire hooks and nicking the barb just through the skin at the 'blunt' end of the maggot where the two dark spots are. These are not eyes. This allows plenty of enticing wriggle.

CASTERS

All is not lost, however, when the bait tin is opened and the maggots are found to have turned into chrysalids, known to anglers as casters. This is a bait which can be very effective for roach in winter when the food supply is not of the same level as in summer. Baiting-up with the caster

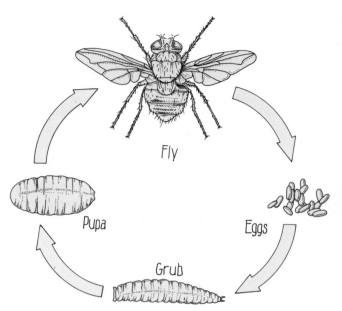

Fly

Eggs

Grub

Pupa

is not as easy as it is with the soft maggot, because underneath the tough, segmented brown shell is nothing but a yellow mush and once the shell is broken there is little left.

When dropped into water, some casters float and some sink in what seems to be a wholly random percentage. The floaters are unwelcome and not taken to the waterside, because if thrown in they will float away on the current and take surface-feeding fish with them. Only use 'sinker' casters as hook or groundbait. The way to hook a caster is to use a very sharp-pointed, fine-wire hook and insert it carefully at the end, leaving the point embedded. It can then be cast in the usual way with an easy underarm flick.

OTHER GRUBS: MEALWORMS, CATERPILLARS, BLOODWORMS

The gardener will often dig up grubs of many species of fly, all of which will make hookbaits. The larvae of the cranefly or daddy-long-legs, popularly known as the leatherjacket, is a real enemy of the gardener and the angler will be welcome if he takes them away for use as bait instead of allowing them to continue their life-cycle. Mealworms are the grubs of a flour beetle and they are sometimes sold in aquaria for tropical-fish food. Again they make an interesting hook bait. The ghost moth lays eggs on nettles and docks, which hatch into larvae called docken grubs. They are worth using as what is called 'sometimes' baits if only because the angler is going through a bad patch and is finding the fish hard to get.

Caterpillars are not the most pleasant of creatures to impale on hooks, but this is a bait for the observant angler. When laden branches over-hang the water and caterpillars are abundant they can sometimes be seen dropping off into the mouths of waiting chub. Now is the moment for this bait to be put to good use and a caterpillar, hooked just below the head so that it retains plenty of movement, may well bring a very nice chub to the waiting net.

It is a pity that the bloodworm is so named because it is not a worm, it is the larva of the tiny midge which gathers in clouds over the water at times. This is a bait that has a large following among anglers who are prepared to suffer for their sport. The reason for this is that bloodworms are rarely if ever offered for sale and therefore must be gathered. Their habitat is stagnant mud which is not the most pleasant place for a stroll. The larvae are scraped off the surface with tools which have to be made at home and are rather like hockey-sticks with extra-long blades. The blade is drawn across the top of the mud and the bloodworms collect on the front edge from where they are removed and dropped on to damp peat. Hooking a bloodworm is yet another problem and the traditional method is to lay the larva on the ball of the thumb and gently introduce the point of a very fine, tiny hook along the body of the bloodworm.

There is also an even smaller hookbait called the joker, and the joke is on the angler. This is the larva of the gnat and its wriggles are out of all proportion to its diminutive size. Both the bloodworm and the joker are excellent fish-catchers live, but they are not easy to obtain and very difficult to mount.

ABOVE Bread is both a cheap and highly successful lure for fish.

WORMS

Worms have always been an angler's favourite, but your author has often wondered why, since it cannot be that many worms (or maggots for that matter, but they can fall off carcasses into the water) will be present naturally in water, at least not in sufficient numbers so that fish will be conditioned to accepting them as a normal part of their food. But worms catch fish, so anglers will use them as bait.

While there are about 20 species of worm in Britain, there are three worms that can be dug up or found in the average garden or open ground. The largest is the lobworm, which can be found up to some 8in (20cm) long and can be dug up at almost any time. It is responsible for leaving those spiral heaps on the carefully tended lawn, to the disgust of the gardener and the delight of the angler. It is a bait which again has caught vast numbers of fish and because it is so big it resists the attentions of small, nuisance shoal-fish until the big roach, tench or chub comes along. It should be hooked so that it is held out and retains its liveliness. The two-hook Pennell rig is ideal for holding worms attractively.

Collecting the lobworm is often best accomplished at night, when the worm comes to the surface. A sprinkling of water often induces them to rise and appear on the surface, when they can be gripped and held until the body bristles on each segment are relaxed, when the creature can be pulled free. Any over-eager pull usually means half a worm in the fingers, the missing 50 per cent will retreat and proceed to grow another front half.

Next comes the brandling, smaller than the lobworm and easily recognisable because of the yellow rings or bands which line the body segments and exude a pungent mucus. This may account for the way fish fall to it. This worm lives in rotting vegetable material and compost-heaps.

Found in the same substrate as the brandling, the redworm does not have the distinctive banded segments as the brandling but has a darker coloration. It is as effective as a hook bait.

Any other kind of worm found by the angler can be put on the hook. Marshworms, for instance, can be dug out of riverbanks and since they fall naturally into the water they are well detected and accepted by fish.

Like maggots, worms can be bred by the angler keen to supply his own bait. In the case of worms, the process is not in any way unpleasant. All that is needed is a compost heap and any worm you dig up in the garden can be introduced to it, although any free-lying compost heap will have its own natural worm colony.

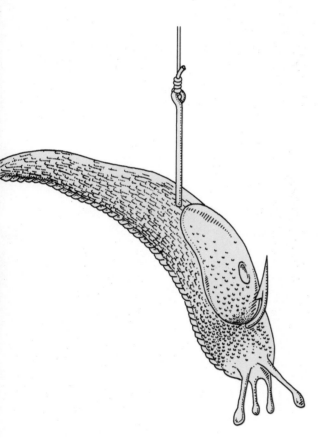

SLUGS

To the gardener the slug is a pest to be destroyed whenever seen lying bloated after dining on prize flowers. There are some 20 species and the angler does the gardener a favour when he collects them for bait. The large black, the grey and the red slugs are best because most of the other species are minute. As with all baits the slugs used must match the hook size and the point pushed through the rear end of the creature. Big slugs are weighty enough to be cast free-line out to where chub might be lying and if one drops on the fish's nose it is almost certain to take it immediately.

BREAD

Anybody who has dropped small pieces of bread into the domestic goldfish bowl knows that the fish's reaction will be to waste no time in grabbing it. There is no doubt about the value of bread as a bait for many species of freshwater fish (and, as it happens, harbour mullet). Bread in all its variations can be put to use. It is also the main ingredient of groundbait mixes. By no means the least of its attractions is that it is cheap; apart from naturally available baits such as worms, insects and hedgerow fruits it is possibly the cheapest.

BREAD FLAKE

Any book about coarse fishing is certain to expound on the value of flake as a known winner for bream and roach. It is simple to put on the hook. Take any hook between Size 12 and 16 or thereabouts, a short-shank round-bend model, pull a piece of flake from the centre of a fresh loaf (some say sliced, wrapped bread is best because it stays moist longer) and just pinch it on to the shank. Leave the point exposed and the squeezed part will hold during the cast. As the bread expands in the water, small pieces will break away to attract fish near to the hookbait.

BREAD PASTE

This treatment of the inside of the loaf makes a rather more compact bait which can be worked into small balls and pushed on to the hook. A danger is that if the paste is too tacky and the point hidden a fish can take the bait but the point does not work and the fish rejects the paste when it feels resistance.

For paste the bread must be a few days old. The crust is cut away and the bread put in water until it is well soaked. Then take some clean rag, place the sodden bread in it and squeeze the water out, kneading the bread into a smooth consistency. If there is time, some anglers take their bread to the water and make their paste there, the reason being that it will contain the 'smell' of the water where the fish are instead of tap-water which will contain chemicals and is therefore alien to the fish's body chemistry.

CRUST

This form of bread bait is not just the hard, crackly outer part of a loaf. It is that, but with some of the firmer, inner crumb attached. Cut slices through the crust and press them between a damp cloth. This has the effect of compressing the outer to the inner parts of the crust and giving an attractive, floating bait. Cut into cubes of the appropriate size for the species being fished for the floating crust makes really exciting fishing.

BREADPUNCH

This really useful little gadget makes the production of compact bread pellets very easy. A small tube, which is available with detachable heads of varying sizes, is pressed on to the bread and the hook can be mounted before the small cylinder of bread is lifted away. By this means the fingers never need to touch the bait. The breadpunch can also be used for making small pieces of groundbait so that a sprinkling – but *only* a sprinkling – of very tasty items of bread can be sown to keep the fish interested.

CHEESE

It is difficult to state why cheese should be a very useful hookbait for cyprinids, but it has taken many very fine chub, barbel and roach. Why these fish accept it is just another of the bait mysteries, for cheese cannot form part of the natural underwater food experienced by fish. The main reason must be the smell which cheese gives off. In order to stay on the hook, cheese must be fresh. Once it is stale and hardened it becomes crumbly but it is still of use to the angler. Grate it, then mix it in with the groundbait, but be sparing because groundbait is not intended to provide a good meal for the fish, its function is to give them just enough to expect more, and that more also contains a hook.

The cheeses which make good baits are the firm Cheddars, Gloucesters

LEFT Minnows make very useful dead-baits. They can be netted or collected in a minnow-trap. This small fish is ideal as a bait for perch and chub.

and Red Leicester, but processed cheeses and 'smellies' also work when moulded on to the hook. The size of the bait will be dictated by hook size and this, of course, by the fish species being fished for. The large mouth of the chub and barbel can accommodate quite large pieces of cheese, while roach will need much smaller baits.

SEEDS

There are many seed baits which have been used by anglers, some of which were in common use but are now fairly unusual. The best known is the notorious hemp, once thought to have a narcotic effect on fish, making them easier to catch! Nonsense of course, but bad news hangs about. Hemp has no ill-effects on fish, to the contrary it has good food value, which is why so many specimen roach fall to it. It is such a winning bait that the National Federation of Anglers for a while banned it from their matches.

Hemp is bought 'rough' and has to be prepared by boiling until the case is softened and splits and the white kernel pops out. Some soda in the water blackens the case and makes a better contrast with the tiny white shoot. The bait must be pressed onto a small hook with a flattened end and since it has the appearance and shape of the old lead split-shot weight should be kept further up from the hook. Hemp can be used as groundbait but only sparingly, for it can fill fish stomachs and that is not the job of groundbait.

A word of warning: do not decide to grow your own hemp seed by planting the grains in the garden. The result will be a large plant known better as the raw material for cannabis!

SWEETCORN

Some 20 years ago an angler opened a tin of sweetcorn, put one of the yellow grains on a hook and cast it out. It caught fish, and thus started yet another popular-bait fashion, but one that has lasted since it really is an excellent bait for cyprinids. Tench particularly fall to sweetcorn (it used to be called 'maize') when put on a Size 10 hook.

TARES

Whatever 'tares' are, weeds seeds, grass seeds, mustard seeds, any unwanted seeds after grain has been riddled, they used to be employed as bait on waters where the dreaded hemp had been banned. Like hemp, they must be boiled and softened before a Size 14 hook will hold them securely.

WHEAT, RICE AND BARLEY

All these grains are working baits, once standard offerings by anglers and the grain size must be matched by an appropriate hook. Rice is small and so it has had success when offered as a free-falling bait for surface-feeding dace.

VEGETABLES: POTATOES, BEANS, PEAS

These fairly large baits have all been used as change-baits when the standard maggot or bread was being ignored, and no doubt fish have fallen to them. Most have to be softened just enough to have the hook pushed into them, or a baiting needle inserted and the line threaded through. Then the hook is attached and pulled tight, with the barb free. Richard Walker was the man who made par-boiled potatoes famous as a carp bait and again we have to ask: how many carp are used to boiled potatoes for lunch instead of browsing on small insects, plant detritus and the like? But potatoes catch fish.

MEATS

In the 1950s and 60s, when food counters were recovering and being stocked with exotic goodies, anglers were experimenting with things that were novel when thought of as baits. Corned-beef was one, and cut into cubes and legered proved quite useful for chub. Luncheon-meat, too, attracted barbel, as did sausage meat and some of the 'smellie' Continental sausages. There is a danger that almost any bait when used exclusively for too long will be ignored, the reason possibly being that if fish are hooked regularly on one thing they become conditioned to seeing it as a threat.

HIGH-PROTEIN BAITS

The history of this branch of special baits begins with the specimen-hunting fanatics who constantly sought that perfect, never-fail bait which would bring fame and fortune to the captor of a new record, preferably something like a huge carp. These baits were made from all kinds of 'secret' ingredients and the angler would spend hours bent over the cooker like an alchemist seeking the recipe for gold, concocting baits which we now call 'boilies'. The ingredients include wheatgerm health foods, yeast, stock cubes in different flavours, casein all or some of which are mixed with eggs and turned into balls and boiled. But a Master Chef's Diploma is no longer necessary before the angler can bit up with boilies, because the tackle trade has seen the profitability of boilies and sells them in many different sizes, flavours and textures.

NATURAL ANIMAL BAITS

Crayfish, freshwater mussel, shrimps, flies. These creatures all come within the experience of fish and so will be eaten when sizable. Chub are probably the only cyprinids that will take crayfish although barbel are reported to do so, but this crustacean needs pure flowing waters which sadly are becoming fewer and fewer, so much so that conservation orders exist in some places for this small lobster-like animal. It is best to say that crayfish should not be used as bait while their numbers are dwindling.

Freshwater mussels, on the other hand, are not in decline. There is more than one species, but the largest, called the swan mussel, is most used as a bait. The animals are raked out from the shallows and placed in buckets of water. When needed, the shell is opened opposite the hinge with a stout blade (the ordinary penknife blade is too weak) and the creature scooped out. The only fleshy part, the 'foot', is hooked and as this is a biggish bait for large fish, a No. 6 hook is best.

Many flies both aquatic and terrestrial are found on and over water and can be mounted on small hooks. Daddy-long-legs, bees, wasps (be careful when handling them!) and grasshoppers are all useful. There are special hooks which have sprung bars for holding flies, but they can be placed on small hooks and free-lined on the surface, where dace and rudd will come up to them.

PLANTS AND FRUITS

When fishing the enticing white-water of a weir there is an old favourite bait that can be collected on the spot, it is silkweed. The trick with this bait is that it is not 'hooked' in the understood sense, but strands are

ABOVE The two-hook Jardine snap-tackle dates back many years but is a highly effective dead-bait mount using bleak. The snap-tackle is suitable for larger baits than minnow. It takes pike and perch.

folded round the bend, leaving tendrils free to weave and flap in the current. Fish will take the weed itself, but others nudge and worry the weed in search of the insect life it carries and so are hooked in the process.

Many berries fall off bankside vegetation, some of which are taken by fish. Those generally used by anglers are blackberries, elderberries and cherries, which have had the stones removed first.

FISH BAITS: LIVEBAITS AND DEADBAITS

It has always been part of angling's long tradition that fish will catch fish, so are acceptable as bait whether dead or alive. Today, we are beginning to understand the natural reluctance of many people to use a live creature in this way and so livebaiting is declining. It can be argued that nature has no such feelings and that our attitude is anthropomorphic – in other words we attribute human fears and traumas to other creatures which cannot experience such feelings. The old truism 'Nature red in tooth and claw' sums it up, but perhaps we are not given rights to subject animals to the predations of others. Man is enough of a predator already!

Deadbaiting is another matter and perfectly acceptable. This method has accounted for huge numbers of very large pike, zander, perch, catfish, eels and probably other species which are not known as scavengers or carnivores. There are many species of small coarse fish which form deadbaits: gudgeon, bleak, minnow, small roach, bullhead, rudd, bream and even sticklebacks and elvers.

There are well-tried mounts for small deadbaits, the two-hook Pennell and three-hook Stewart rigs holding small fish securely so that they wobble and turn when being retrieved while spinning. The Jardine snap-tackle is another old and well-tried method of presenting a deadbait. For perch, the smaller fish can be lip-hooked. But freshwater fish are not the only ones the coarse angler has at his disposal. On the fishmonger's slab are herring, mackerel, sprats and all take the hungry pike. Whole herring, sometimes injected with fish oils, are cast out to lay on the bottom waiting for the pike to home-in on the scent. The heads of mackerel, with the guts left hanging are also used for the same purpose.

So far as baits are concerned, the angler is recommended to try anything remotely edible. The unusual offering has been known to surprise even the most experienced angler.

Accessories

The non-angler, seeing your keen fisherman trudging along the river-bank looking like a paratrooper at Tumbledown and laden with holdalls, box, bait-cans, pockets bulging and bits of paraphernalia hanging from his shoulders, must wonder what on earth is needed to get the angler started. The following items are not comprehensive, just sufficient!

LANDING-NET

Not all fish need to be led over the rim of a landing-net — 'scooped' is absolutely the wrong word — for some are small and light enough to be lifted from the water to be unhooked. When bigger fish are encountered, those large and strong enough to pull hard and take line off the reel before they have been played out and can be drawn in, the wise angler uses a landing-net.

This necessary accessory can be a simple handled, round frame with a mesh net, but it can also be a good deal more sophisticated. This is fine for the average fish, but the net should not be plunged into the water and the fish scooped out, sizable fish should be drawn over the waiting, just-submerged rim. This way the fish is not likely to be scared into one last thrash which can break the line. In that case you can put the net down and start again. Furthermore, triangular nets are an improvement; with the flat side at the front, this aids the smooth netting of specimen fish.

Landing-nets can be bought with extending handles which double the average 4ft length. Some have a metal spike at the end of the handle for sticking into the river or lake-bed when the angler is wading but needs the net to hand. It is no use wondering where you have left the net when your rod is bucking and bending under the surges of a fish which will definitely need netting. The netting itself once used to be made of very rough cord, which easily harmed the fish as it struggled. Now, soft but strong nylon is used which does not rot as did the old material.

ANGLERS' BOXES

The traditional angler's box was a wicker basket with a large leather hinge and once the reel, bait-boxes, hook-wallets, floats, accessories, lunch, and towels for wet hands, were removed the angler sat on it to a chorus of creaks and groans and began fishing. But riverside mud and damp soon got into the wicker and it began to degenerate. The modern angler is equipped either with a large, strong plastic box-seat or one with a canvas-covered metal frame. These are virtually rot-proof but one problem affects the metal-framed seats: their weight tends to sink them into the ground where it is soft and muddy. Boxes can carry much of what the angler needs, but his rods, landing net, keep-net, bank-sticks, and umbrella all have to be slung over shoulders or toted in some other way. Within the angler's main box-seat will be various other containers for bait, hooks, weights and so on. His floats need special care for some are fragile, so float-boxes with different-sized compartments can be bought or made from cigar boxes by the handyman.

DISGORGERS

These are used to remove the hooks from fishes' mouths and in the wrong or clumsy hands are often nothing more than cruel and barbaric instruments. The common type is a metal rod. To remove a hook, one end has a notch which is pushed against the barb of the hook in the fish's mouth to release it. The theory is fine, but in practice the disgorger is poked about and the fish suffers quite improper injury. The modern,

ABOVE The static angler must have all his necessary gear within reach and not scattered round him. The wicker seat-basket is rapidly disappearing in favour of plastic models.

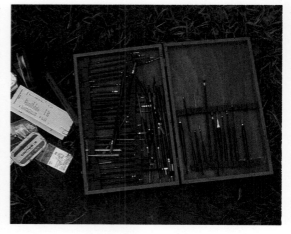

ABOVE Floats for almost every wind and water situation can be kept in boxes such as these. Many floats are fragile and this method keeps them safe from the clumsy wader. It is not likely that anywhere near this number of floats will be needed at one session.

RIGHT A triangular landing-net being used in the correct way. The lip of the net is kept steady below the surface as the fish is drawn over it. Only then is the net lifted from the water.

caring angler now carries a proper surgical instrument with him in the form of artery forceps which grip the hook-bend so that the hook can be gently pushed free and removed.

In the case of large pike, with their formidable canine teeth, it was the fashion to use either a stick to wedge between the fish's jaws and keep them open or to use a horrid gadget called a gag, which was placed between the top and lower jaws of the pike. The ends were held apart by a spring, usually causing injury to the lining of the pike's mouth. Now a great deal more consideration is shown to all fish species and the forceps make hook removal easy and clean.

CATAPULTS

Old-timers became very adept at throwing their large balls of bread-crumb groundbait out to where the shoal was waiting. This was not difficult due to the consistency of the mixture, but when the groundbait was thinner it tended to break up in flight so that it was distributed in a line between the angler and the fish – not what the angler intended or wanted. It was the late Richard Walker, I think, who suggested that if the groundbait was mixed with grass and mud from the riverbank it could be thrown without falling apart in mid-air. It was virtually impossible to throw a handful of maggots or casters so that it remained intact when it hit the water.

Then an angling genius, perhaps confiscating his son's window-breaking catapult, suddenly realized that this was the answer. The forked, rubber-powered catapult was taken to the waterside and with a little practice the angler was able to project particle baits with real accuracy. The specialized angling catapult has a cup or pouch which holds the bait tidily while the angler takes aim, then lets fly and the contents are sent straight and true out to the intended spot.

HOLDALLS

Rods in their bags, landing-net handles and umbrellas, and bank-sticks can be rolled into weatherproof holdalls which make carrying easier. They also have handy smaller pockets for the many little things which make an angler's life easier; things which he never needs until the moment comes when he realizes that he left them at home.

UMBRELLAS

The angler has no use for the conventional domestic umbrella. Although it will keep the rain off, it is not strong enough, cannot be stuck into the ground, and the handle cannot be angled to keep off wind as well as rain. The material used for the angler's umbrella is much thicker than the home-type, for it must withstand hard use and the buffeting of heavy rain and wind. The umbrella's capacity for wind-protection is just as import-ant as its rain-proof material, for there is not much more misery-inducing than cold and wet fingers when tiny hooks have to be tied to gossamer-thickness nylon, or reel-line has to be threaded through the small rings of a long, whippy match-rod. There are umbrellas which have lugs round the rim so that it can be held down by guy-ropes.

KEEP-NETS

Keep-nets were once a common sight wherever coarse anglers fished. However these accessories are becoming increasingly unpopular with the exception of fishing matches where the total bag of each competitor is weighed to find the winner. The trouble with keep-nets is that it is wrong

ABOVE The pouch of an angling catapult being filled with hemp. Catapults give remarkable accuracy in placing particle groundbaits exactly where they are needed, impossible by any other means.

to confine numbers of fish in them. The netting material used to be of harsh twine or hard nylon, both of which materials caused injury to tail-fins and rubbed scales off the fishes' bodies, removing the mucus and allowing the entry of parasites and disease. If the water is shallow there will not be enough depth to keep all the fish moderately comfortable; if the weather is hot the water can quickly become de-oxygenated and the fish will die; if predators are in the area they can be attracted to the fishes' movements in the net and attack them.

Where they are necessary, keep-nets must have a mesh of a statutory size, and have a top-ring measurement of a minimum diameter. They should also be long enough to allow the fish room to move, remembering that on most occasions the top ring of the net will need to stand out of the water. Where possible make sure that the net is extended and running along the current, not simply hanging in a heap straight down.

ABOVE As well as match-anglers, many anglers use a bait-tray so that 'special' hook-maggots can be to hand as well as feeders. The catapult is also handy for placing feeder maggots in the correct spot.

ROD-RESTS

Stuck into the ground, a suitably stout forked twig is fine as a rod stick but it has its limitations: unless the vee of the fork is just right the line running along the bottom of the rod will be trapped and could mean a lost fish when the resistance was felt. Used correctly, the commercial model, with the vee shaped so that the line runs freely beneath the rod, is used in pairs so that the rod can be supported horizontally. This allows the angler to sit comfortably with his hand ready to lift the rod and strike in one motion.

When legering in windy conditions and to avoid line being pushed into a large bow, making a strike difficult if not impossible, it is useful to have the rod-tip just below the water surface. Here, the leading rod-rest is pushed farther into the ground so that the rod dips at the correct angle. There are times, too, when rods can be sited so that they are parallel to the bank. Bites are registered much more obviously because the line then runs out at right-angles to the rod.

BAIT-STANDS

The matchman's fishing time is limited and he is concerned with wasting no time during the match. 'A dry hook catches no fish!' is the old saying. This means he must have everything close to hand, and the bait-stands help by having different hook-baits within quick reach. The large feeder-maggot bucket or groundbait container must also be close-by.

BITE INDICATORS

One of the simplest bite detectors is a small ball of bread-paste pressed on to the line between reel and first rod ring. Its weight pulls the line down and when a bite occurs the vee suddenly straightens and the angler strikes. Because it is only pressed on gently, the ball of bread-paste flies off without affecting the playing of the fish. Another old favourite is a piece of flattened silverpaper hung over the line, but there is ample room for ingenuity in inventing simple but effective bite alarms.

'Progress' and the tackle manufacturers have produced many kinds of mechanical bite detectors, which range from simple hooks dangling from the line between the reel and first rod ring, to highly sophisticated electronic buzzers, some of which have flashing lights as well. The Salmon and Freshwater Fisheries Act 1923 states that it is an offence 'to use any light for the purpose of taking salmon, trout or freshwater fish'. The use of lights on electronic alarms to announce bites does not seem to contravene the Act, nor does shining a torch on to a float during the hours of darkness.

SWIM-FEEDERS AND BAIT-DROPPERS

Swim-feeders and bait-droppers comprise two of the great advances in coarse angling and matchfishing in particular. The exact placing of groundbait and loose-feed when legering is very important and while catapulted and hand-thrown mixtures can be placed well enough these accessories do it much better. They also have a big bonus in that one does not need a leger weight, for a strip of lead runs down the side of the container.

The swim-feeder is a weighted, perforated, open-ended tube which can be packed with groundbait that works its way out as the container lies on the bed. Bait-droppers are a little more complicated in that one end is closed with a simple hatch and particle loose-feed such as maggots, casters, hemp and so on is put in and the lid is shut. The bait-dropper is swung out and lowered to the fishing area, where as it touches bottom the lid opens and deposits the groundbait where it is needed.

HOOK SHARPENER

Many anglers accept hooks without making sure that they have the right temper and the point is sharp. Temper can be tested by pressing the

ABOVE The tray of this dial-scale has a loose lid which is rested on the fish to prevent them from flopping about and injuring their fins. This is a weigh-in after a match on the Pevensey Levels, Sussex.

RIGHT Pan scales will carry less weight than dial scales. The pan is shallow, without a cover so the fish may flop out. In the dish is a perch and some roach.

point gently on to the thumbnail and assessing the hook's springiness. If at fault and the hook snaps it is discarded. But a blunt hook can be missed – and so can the fish. All the angler needs is a small whetstone or carborundum with which to touch up the point of the hook when needed.

WEIGHING YOUR FISH

Unless the fish is an exceptional specimen, or you are weighing-in at the end of a match, there is not much use for scales. There are four kinds of scales, those with a dial, those with a pan, beam scales, and spring balances. Machinists have to be checked accurately, and here the beam scales are used, but for casual use (and for ease of transportation) the simple spring balance is adequate. These will not give total accuracy, but do supply a very close reading which if necessary can be checked later if the angler feels he has a record-breaking fish.

CAMERA

At this point the angler might well have a camera with him. This is not only for the personal pleasure in having a visual record of the fish. If the fish is a newsworthy one, the angling press will be interested and a published photograph does wonders for the angler's ego!

PLUMMET

Unless the swim is familiar to the angler, he may not know the depth of the water there and so is not able to adjust the length of line between the float and the hook. Depth can be checked by the use of a plummet, a small cone-shaped weight with a strip of cork at the base and an eye at the top. The hook on the reel line is threaded through the eye and the point nicked gently into the cork. When this is lowered into the swim a free-running float will find its level on the surface while the plummet lies on the bottom. This shows the depth and the angler can adjust the float accordingly.

CLOTHING

While not strictly an accessory, the angler's clothing while fishing is very important. He must be warm and dry from head to foot in all weathers, winter and summer. A sudden heavy shower can ruin an enjoyable fishing trip if the angler is not prepared; a slip or stumble at the water's edge can leave the feet wet and cold if proper waterproof boots or shoes are not being worn. 'Wellies' will sometimes be adequate, but not smooth-soled ones where there is mud or any slippery surface. Woollen gloves can be a mistake too, once wet they remain so and tend to keep fingers cold. Mittens of some kind made of a waterproof wool, leaving the fingers free, can keep the hands fairly warm. Most anglers need to sit at some time, but wet grass or mud is not conducive to health if the trousers are not waterproof. Lastly, hats can be the emblem of the fisherman, festooned with flies and club badges. They will also keep the head warm and in fly fishing they will protect the ear from a wayward cast and prevent a fast-moving hook from finding a painful lodging in an ear-lobe.

FOOD AND DRINK

A long day's fishing can be tiring and most anglers breakfast very early before setting out. Twelve hours away is not unusual and so some kind of sustenance is necessary. Drink is best confined to something non-alcoholic, if only because the angler might be driving home and we all know the importance of not drinking and driving.

FLY FISHING

 To be a fly fisherman is both a joy and an affliction. Few more testing yet delightful ways of catching a fish exist, and no one would choose to hunt their food in such a way if survival was their main obsession. There are many easier ways to catch fish, especially a creature as cussed as a salmon or downright dumb as a trout. Fly casting is an efficient way to get a bait to a fish. Flies, imitative, or even designed to infuriate are an unlikely way to simulate a living creature when the living creature could often be impaled on a hook, and cast with fine monofilament and a reel after a few minutes tuition.

The fly fisherman can trace his roots to a very different age, when the long whip-like rod and tapered line would be the only way to flick out a fly. His method should long ago have been superseded, instead it thrives and grows, with ever more converts to the sport becoming entranced with its pleasures. Fly fishing is not merely a sport, it is an art, one in which keenness of eye and control of hand are vital. The fly-fisherman's canvas is the water, his critics are the trout, and his rewards blessedly tangible. For the rise, the take, the pull and the battle of the trout, salmon, or any sporting fish are all more pleasurable when fly tackle is used than with almost any other fishing method.

It is a year-round pursuit too, and not just because so many different species may fall to the lure of a fly. Tackle care and, more to the point, flydressing and the study of entomology become essential parts of the full enjoyment of the sport. Winter evenings indoors are never dull, there is always work for idle hands, and even the least dexterous can produce wisps of fur and feather that will deceive the craftiest trout.

At first, the skills are easily mastered, but the full lesson is never learnt. Trout, salmon and lunker pike make no differentiation between novice and expert. The well-presented fly conquers all, and if at first that presentation lacks finesse, there will be younger, less tutored, perhaps downright stupid fish to oblige.

The following chapters open the doors to the kindergarten class, but the full lesson will take a pleasurable lifetime by the water, and yet never be fully learnt.

Fly Fishing Tackle

Fly fishing differs from all other forms of angling in that the line provides the casting weight. It is the secret of presenting a tiny, near weightless fly, to a fish at distances of up to 50yd (46m).

To get this method of casting to work at its best great casting skills are necessary (to be discussed later), but balanced tackle is also required. What is meant by balanced? All fly rods and fly lines are rated by AFTMA numbers so that they can be perfectly matched for casting performance. A #7 rod will work with a #7 line, although it is not quite as simple as that, because the rod will in fact work with the first 30ft (9m) of that #7 line.

Lines are available from about a #3 up to a #13. Of course, there are rods to match, and some of them will not be graded for just one line but two, perhaps even three. So you might see a #7–to–#8 rod, but with the superb graphite rods available these days this need not concern the beginner. As a novice, err to the heavier side and choose an #8 line. The question of which weight and length of rod, matched to which weight of line, is needed to catch fish with a fly will be discussed shortly.

First, though, let's take a look in turn at rods, and lines, and try to establish just what you need to look for when buying them.

RODS

Rods are available in three main materials – glassfibre, graphite (carbon fibre), or bamboo (split-cane). Graphite is the best material currently available for the vast majority of fly rods, so the others can be disposed of quickly.

Glassfibre is now refined to perfection. Rods in this material are durable, slightly heavier than graphite, and generally less stiff. Consequently you need a broader cross-section on a glass rod, and even then it will lack the accuracy and crispness of graphite. However, it is an excellent material for slow-actioned shorter rods, and quite nice for heavy-duty ocean fly fishing. Bamboo is constructed from split sections of bamboo, glued and joined to form a six-sided rod. Building such weapons is craftsman's work, and the finished item is a thing of beauty. Split-cane, far heavier than man-made fibres, is very accurate due to its flat-sided construction, and a joy to fish with on small streams. It also handles fish well, and sets hooks home soundly. But over 8ft (2.5m) it becomes cumbersome – and is very expensive. So, for everyday fishing, graphite has to be the choice. In the ten or so years it has been available it has revolutionized fly rod construction; light and durable unless hit hard from the side, with intelligent rod design it can be supplied with almost any conceivable action.

At the bottom of the rod, there will be a reel seat, preferably one that tucks the reel up under the hand rather than leaving it wobbling at the bottom of the rod, and a handle, which will generally be of cork. It would be nice if rod handles were left unfinished so that the angler could shape them to his own design. Sadly this is not the case, and it is advisable to try several different shapes to find the one that suits you.

Your rod will have guides – rod rings – of one of two sorts. The first is the classic snake guide. Made of wire, it is light, flexible, and these days usually of durable and corrosion-proof metal. These rings are highly recommended, except in areas where they will be subjected to constant wear through double-hauling or if used on a gritty bank, when the second type of ring, a more solid type with a 'liner' of very hard material such as silicone carbide, is preferable. There are two minor drawbacks to this type of ring; the first is that they create a lot of friction on the line when casting, which will reduce distance, and they are also heavier and less flexible than snake rings. To compensate, they virtually never need changing.

Rods are available in lengths from 5ft (1.5m) to the British salmon rod of up to 20ft (6m). However, the vast majority of normal fly fishing will be done with rods from 8 to 10ft (2.5–3m), with 9ft (2.7m) being a useful compromise and all-round length. Few long-distance tournament casters feel the need for a rod longer than 10ft (3m), and rod length has little effect on casting distance when compared with choice and profile of line.

Later we will describe five basic outfits for all fly fishing – but following these guidelines the beginnner will be well-equipped for small to quite large rivers, and most still-waters, with a carbon rod of 9–9½ft (2.7–2.9m) long, equipped with snake guides, and possibly a silicone carbide or similar ring at the butt to take the added stress and friction of casting. This rod will be rated for a particular weight of fly line. Which weight is a good compromise for the novice armed with this rod, will be discussed shortly, but first, to clarify the choice of line weights, and

ABOVE A selection of internationally available fly lines for the modern fisherman, including sinkers, slow sinkers, floaters and sink-tips. Most are coated with PVC, although Airflo lines are covered with a tougher polymer coating.

indeed of any fly line, an explanation of the fly line itself is needed.

FLY LINES
PROFILES AND SINKING RATES

Modern fly lines are constructed with a plastic coat of PVC over a Terylene core. The plastic can be distributed on to the core in a taper so that it results in a line 'profile'. However, 'modern' is a relative term. Twenty years ago fly lines were commonly made of silk, but now PVC line has taken over completely — which is not to say that it is the ultimate fly line. Time will tell if the new polymer coating on the Kevlar-core fly lines will live up to their manufacturer's many promises, and replace the old-style line. My feeling is that, like silk, the old PVC line will survive for many years, since it has some advantages over the new lines.

Back to basics — what profiles do the manufacturers build into their fly lines? There are two basic types, double-taper (which as the name suggests has a taper at each end), and forward-taper or weight-forward (where instead of a line with an even taper at both ends, the main casting weight is at the front end). Now (as you have read), the first 30ft (9m) of the line supplies the correct casting weight for the rod. So a gently tapering 30ft (9m) of double-taper (and in practice some level centre section) will weight a matched rod, and must be moved through the air to cast.

On a forward-taper, however, the casting weight in the form of that belly is pushed up nearer the front of the line, and in aerializing 30ft (9m) of line, you are not only making the rod work perfectly, but also getting all of the 'thick bit' of the line outside the tip ring of the rod. Now, by single or double-hauling to get more line speed you can cast out this belly, with nothing but the resistance of fine running-line or back taper to slow your cast.

Try the same with a double-taper line, and you have a lot of thick belly line resisting your efforts. So why bother with a double-taper line at all? Well, apart from the obvious benefit that you can reverse the line and use the other end when one end wears out, a double-taper line used for short casts can present a fly far more delicately than a forward-taper, which has a more gradual taper from a fine tip. It is also more accurate.

SHOOTING-HEADS

The logical development therefore is the shooting-head. Why not cut off the first 30ft (9m) of a double-taper and smoothly join it to fine running line (usually monofilament such as 30lb (13.5kg) Stren)? That 30ft (9m) can then be cast further, without losing the fine tip and presentation. Now take the proposition even further: if it is hard work to aerialize 30ft (9m) of fly line, why not cut the shooting-head from a line one or two sizes heavier? A shorter length will still make the rod work. Perhaps 20ft (6m) of #9 fly line will work with a #7-rated rod. The resultant line is called a shooting-head and with its many variations it is the weapon for long-casting — though the principle of improved presentation relies on considerable casting skills.

So the line profile the angler chooses will depend on his venue. Small rivers and tiny ponds require double-taper lines, all short-casting situations are better met with them. Larger rivers and still-waters in general will probably call for a forward-taper. Shooting-heads are handy for all long-range work, and are used most often for big river sea-trout, steelhead, single-handed salmon fishing, and, fly fishing at sea, where long casts are often essential.

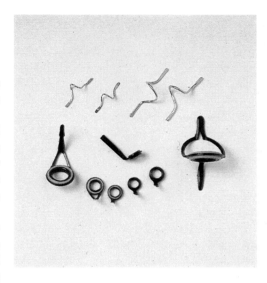

ABOVE Guides (rod rings) for the modern rod; snake rings (top) and hard-lined Fuji's (below).

FLOATING AND SINKING LINES

Fly lines can be constructed to do everything from floating high to sinking like a stone. There are a variety of methods of achieving this, from incorporating air into the coating to adding metals, either ground-up in the coating, or in the shape of a fine lead-core to the line. However, while the technology need not concern us, the fact that a huge range of fly lines with accurately-rated sinking speeds is available, should. For instance, a line is available that will sink so slowly that it fishes just under the surface film and eliminates line wake; another will sink a foot down on the same retrieve; a third will fish 2ft (.6m) down, and so on. Fly fishermen tend to use vague terms such as fast-sinker, medium-sinker, slow-sinker, intermediate, and neutral-density, without explaining that one manufacturer's slow-sinker is another's medium, and so on.

Various sinking speeds are important for obvious reasons. One is that a very fast sinker will mean less waiting time to fish deep on a stillwater; another is that it might be the only line that will get deep enough in a fast-flowing river. There are less obvious reasons, too. Consider side-casting from a drifting boat. If your partner locates fish at a certain depth (perhaps by counting down his line), you may need exactly the same line to reach those fish. Not only that, but the same profile of line, and the same casting distance from the side of the boat. In short, carrying a range of lines helps you to cope with factors beyond your control.

The novice river angler may need no more than a floating line for 99 per cent of the time; the stillwater man is better equipped with a floater, fast-sinker, and neutral-density or intermediate in that order; the angler who fishes for salmon and steelhead may need a whole range of shooting heads. One last note on fly lines. On occasions a mixed line can pay dividends. There are commercially produced lines with a sinking-tip section of perhaps 10ft (3m), on a floating line. These have a role in stillwater nymphing, and can be helpful in holding a wet fly down when casting downstream and across on rivers. They can also be homemade by joining two sections, or spare pieces of sinking line can be carried and looped on in an emergency. At the other end of the scale, and unavailable commercially, so it must be homemade, comes a float-tip line, which is sometimes handy when fishing deep in snaggy or weedy water to hold a fly up off the bottom.

WHAT WEIGHT?

The novice angler faced with lines from #3 to #13 could be forgiven for panicking. However, compromise comes in the middle of the range, and a line weight of #6 or #7 will be adequate for all but the largest and smallest waters. For heavy work and long-casting you can use a weight-forward #8, or some shooting-heads matched to the rod.

As you progress in both knowledge of fish and casting skill you may well discover the delights of light tackle. A #4 outfit is a joy to use, and because the line has less inertia and the rod less stiffness, far lighter tippets may be used.

REELS

A line needs to be loaded on to a reel and many top fly fishermen use their reels as little more than line reservoirs, playing their fish by hand and not bothering to wind loose line back on to the reel. This presupposes that the hooked fish is not going to make a long run, for if this happens they will be down to the line and backing stored on the reel and light as well take advantage of its facilities.

ABOVE Some of the finest fly reels on the market, from Hardy, Scientific Anglers and the brilliant Dutch craftsman Ari Hart. The reels in the lefthand row are for smaller-stream fishing – although the System Two (second from top) has a superb brake; those in the righthand row are for big-stillwater, steelhead and sea trout fishing.

There are two main types of fly reel, single-action, or multiplying. Single-action reels retrieve one diameter's worth of line for each turn; the spool of a multiplying reel may make three or four rotations for each turn of the handle, which is handy when fish make long runs then turn and come back towards you. For small rivers, and quite a lot of stillwater fishing, single-action reels suffice, and they should be big enough to hold your fly line, plus sufficient backing to cope with any running fish you are likely to encounter. This will vary from 30yd (27m) on small rivers and ponds to 200yd (183m) when hunting salmon, and even more when ocean fishing.

There is a valid argument for using a wide-diameter reel when fishing with a shooting-head, because such a spool puts less of a coil into the backing. Reels are available which feature everything from a simple click drag (which is surprisingly effective at slowing down even quite large trout), to a superb braking mechanism. Every system needs to be suitable for, or sensibly adjusted to, the species of fish you are seeking and the strength of your tippet.

ABOVE Standard tapered and braided leaders, including a fast-sinking braided version.

BACKING

Backing can either be a reservoir of stout line, usually monofilament, or more sophisticated, when used with shooting-heads. Backing is used, quite simply, because a 30yd (27m) fly line does not give room for manoeuvre when playing a big fish.

Shooting head backing is actually cast off the reel and because of this it should be slick and relatively tangle-free. For sinking heads use 30lb (13.5kg) Stren, or a flattened nylon backing; for floaters add grease to the nylon, or use braided backing, which casts superbly. Expensive alternatives are fly-line-style running lines, very fine, and made in floating or sinking forms.

LEADERS AND TIPPETS

At the business end of the fly line, a huge range of leaders is available, made up of gradually descending diameters of neatly knotted braided nylon; they are also available as a tapered weave in one piece. Such leaders can have wire woven into them, or lead wire running through their centres to make them sink. They can be sealed to float, greased to float, or have other materials incorporated into them. These leaders turn over the rest of the tippet well and add a delicate taper to the point of a fly line. They are easy to attach permanently, usually last well and can also be locked in place with a plastic sleeve and quickly changed. In their sinking versions they go a long way to making the sink-tip line redundant, but are a boon to the dry-fly angler when they float well and present the fly accurately. Their construction has a degree of stretch built in too, so there is a cushion against smash takes. All in all they seem useful in lengths up to 4 or 5ft (1–1.5m) as the back taper of a leader. In greater lengths they seem badly troubled by wind, and are more awkward to control in the water than plain nylon. Still, the novice, especially on rivers, should try them, probably in combination with a standard tapered leader, made of tapered monofilament.

They are available with very stiff butts, and in a variety of tippet strengths, colours, and stiffnesses. The novice may make up his own tapered leaders by knotting gradually tapering lengths of nylon, and many formulae for the perfect leader are available.

Most commercially produced leaders are between 9 and 12ft (2.5–3.5m) long, and for stillwater use they need an extra length of

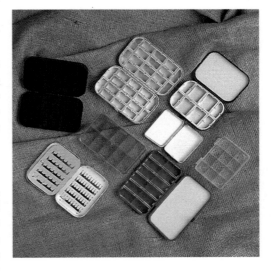

ABOVE Fly boxes range from the simple and inexpensive to the high-priced and immaculate – each one of this range has a role to play.

ABOVE A most useful fishing vest or waistcoat.

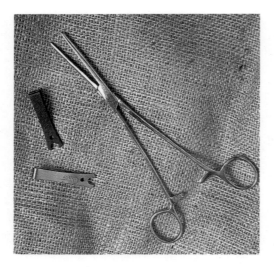

CENTRE Forceps are excellent hook removers and make a useful stream-side fly vice. Clippers ensure neat knots.

BOTTOM Always carry a priest – perhaps incorporating a marrow spoon – to kill your fish.

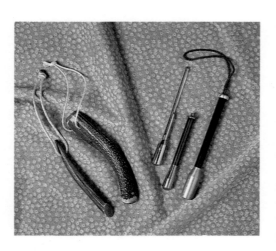

tippet nylon knotted onto them because a longer leader usually brings more takes, or when a dropper is required. Most fly fishermen need to carry tippet nylon from 2 to 8lb (1–3.5kg) breaking strain, with heavier line for big migratory trout, salmon, northern pike and sea fish.

A lot has been said about the colour of nylon, but a nice compromise is to match the tinge of the water: clear for clear water; pale blue in the sea; brown in peaty water; green when algae tinges the water green. However, colour makes little difference if the fly is well-presented.

FLIES

The great essential for success in this sport is the right fly. Notes on choice of fly, fly dressing, and patterns, are given later, but a few guidelines need stressing. There is no point in fishing a superb fly on a terrible hook. The point must be sharp and the temper of the wire perfect. Whether buying hooks with flies ready-tied on them, or tying them yourself, check the hook points.

Artificial flies should also be kept free from rust. Take time after each trip to dry out the flies, and protect fly boxes from rain and damp (although I remember occasions when a rust-dulled tinsel body was more acceptable than a bright flashy one!)

Learn to tie your own flies – it is essential both for economy and for ensuring that you carry sufficient patterns. If you tie your own you can match obscure hatches, ensure that you can always get hold of some more of a killing pattern and copy a friend's successful fly.

Fly boxes should be well made, with reliable closing catches, sound hinges, and should float. If they are brightly coloured, it gives them less chance of being lost. A number of pocket-sized boxes are often more useful than one suitcase-sized one – as long as the contents are clearly labelled. Dry flies, many wet flies, and some nymphs require boxes that will not crush the delicate hackles or legs.

SMALL BUT VITAL

A multi-pocketed fishing waistcoat or vest is usually more useful than a bag for holding what the fly angler needs close to hand, especially when wading. A simple belt pack system is the choice of other anglers. What goes into all those pockets? There are spare shooting-heads, spare fly reels, and reel spools loaded with lines, fly boxes, leaders, and tippet nylon. It should contain the following items, each with a role to play: artery forceps for removing hooks, line clippers with a sharp point for clearing hook eyes and unravelling knots, a weighted cosh for killing fish (called a 'priest'), and a marrow spoon for sampling the stomach contents of dead fish in order to see what it was feeding on. Carry two pairs of polarized sunglasses, a yellow pair for bad light, standard for bright light. These both protect the eyes when casting, and even more important in actual fishing, help you to see fish underwater.

You can also carry a pot of grease like Gunk, to help float the leader and, occasionally, the fly line tip; a sinking agent like Gink, to make the leader sink; a small phial of detergent to degrease your line and fingers before it migrates on to unwanted areas of your tackle; and a bottle of dry-fly proofing, for waterproofing flies.

A large back pocket can accommodate a lightweight waterproof jacket. Some vests also have clips for a net, if required, a rod-holding system which leaves the hands free, and a patch which holds flies securely while they dry. There is a similar band on my favourite fishing hat, and a fly patch on my peaked cap. It is a real disaster if I leave my vest at home!

LEFT Sunglasses both protect the eyes and in practical terms help you spot fish.

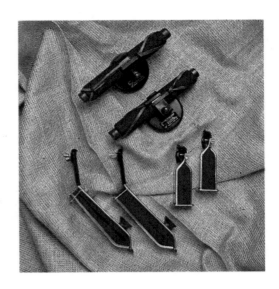

RIGHT Rod holders allow you to carry made-up rods on your car.

LEFT Grease and sinking agents aid fly presentation.

RIGHT Modern or more traditional, the anglers' clothing must be functional

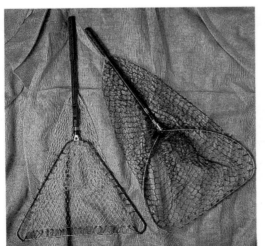

LEFT A good-sized landing net is always useful.

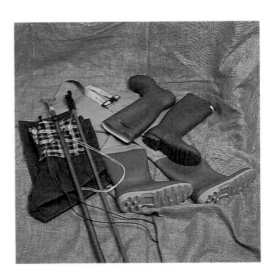

RIGHT Waterproof over-trousers and footwear are equally essential and a wading staff to probe the river bed is a necessary safety item.

CLOTHING

It is impossible to give too many guidelines on clothing as the climate and terrain where game fish are sought varies so much. I would not fly fish without a hat, preferably with a large peak to help keep excess light out from behind my fish-spotting polarized glasses. When wading it is essential to wear clothing that will remain warm when wet, and which dries quickly. Wherever possible, spare dry clothing should be carried. Buy the best waterproof outer clothing you can afford, and err towards the type of clothing preferred by other outdoor sportsmen who put their lives at the risk of the weather – mountaineers for example. Remember, too, that if it is cold on shore it will be colder in a boat on a large water, and icy when wading in the water. Take extra clothing and wear sensible long underwear – several layers are warmer than one big topcoat.

At the other extreme, protect your skin from the sun, and bear in mind that bright sun reflects from water to enhance its rays when you are in a boat or deep wading. Barrier creams, sensible hats and, if necessary, long sleeves, may be essential.

Footwear should be considered in conjunction with temperature, whether wading and whether a slippery river or lake bed requires studs or other grips. Common sense will indicate what you will need. When deep wading, the old-fashioned buoyant wading staff with a rubber-tipped weighted end is still a most useful item.

CARE OF TACKLE

Today's graphite rods need little special care. Wipe them down occasionally and oil any metal reel seat parts. Check the guides for cracks and grooves and the varnish on the whippings. The occasional dab of varnish will keep water out of any cracks, stopping discolouration, and prevent silk whippings from rotting. You must learn how to whip-on a new rod ring. Keep fly lines and all nylon away from sources of heat and sunlight.

Fly lines benefit from an occasional wash in soft soap and a dose of replasticizer. They should also be taken off reels when not in use for a time and loosely coiled. String them out in the open air and give them a good stretch before using them again. Sunlight ruins nylon, and one professional of my acquaintance keeps his stocks in the fridge. It is sound practice to throw nylon away after a season's use, and if a spool shows any signs of poor knot strength, or experiences mysterious breaks, throw it away.

The great enemy of fly reels is grit and dirt. All you need to do is keep them clean, and well-oiled. If you are using a reel that might corrode in saltwater, rinse and dry it thoroughly after use. New reels are sometimes packed with heavy grease, and they generally run smoother if this is removed and some good quality oil substituted. Plenty of WD40 is an effective lazy man's way to maintenance. Flies kept long in storage should be protected from moths and other bugs with a proprietary deterrent; damp fly boxes should be opened and stood over a moderate heat source to dry. If they are stuck on to anything that holds water, such as a woollen fly patch, take them out and dry both patch and flies separately.

Any kind of rubber boot or wader will benefit from storage in a cool, sun-free place, away from electrical switches. Unfold and hang them upside down by the foot. For on-the-bank repairs, nothing beats cyno-acrilate glue, which as will be seen in the next chapter, securely attaches a braided leader.

SMALL STREAMS AND PONDS

- **Quarry:** trout, grayling, panfish, small bass
- **Rod:** 6 to 7ft graphite rod #4
- **Fly line:** floating double-taper line #4 (sometimes #5 or #6 where a short cast is made and less fly line is needed to balance the rod)
- **Leaders:** 6 to 9ft (1.8–2.7m) long
- **Tippets:** up to 4lb (1.8kg)
- **Flies:** small streamers, popping bugs, wet flies, nymphs and dry flies

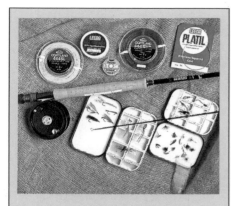

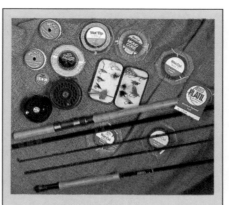

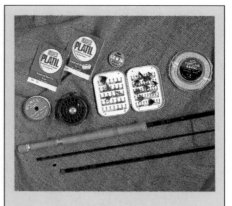

STANDARD OUTFIT – STILLWATER NYMPHING AND LARGE RIVERS

- **Quarry:** trout, grayling, bass, panfish, steelhead, sea trout, northern pike and light sea fishing
- **Rod:** 9 or 9½ft (2.7 or 2.9m) graphite #6 and #7
- **Reel:** single-action or multiplying fly reel with 100yd (91m) of backing; shooting-head backing as required
- **Fly line:** double-taper #6 floater; weight-forward #7 floater; range of sinking weight-forward or shooting-heads as required
- **Leaders:** 9 to 20ft (2.7–6m) long
- **Tippets:** 3 to 8lb (1.4–3.6kg), plus wire where required
- **Flies:** large streamers, popping bugs, full range of wet flies, nymphs and dry flies

HEAVY OUTFIT – LARGE RIVERS, LAKES AND OCEAN FISHING

- **Quarry:** single-handed salmon, steelhead, sea trout, largemouth bass, northern pike and muskellunge, tarpon (small shark)
- **Rod:** 10 or 10½ft (3 or 3.2m) #8 or #9; double-handed European salmon fly rod to 16ft (5m) or more
- **Reel:** very large capacity reel – single-action may be more reliable – with a superb braking system and loaded with 200yd (183m) or more of backing; also shooting-head backing
- **Fly line:** full range of shooting-heads with various sinking speeds; salmon double-hander will require a range of heavy double-taper lines
- **Leaders:** to 20ft (6m)
- **Tippets:** 5 to 15lb (2.2–6.8kg), plus wire trace where necessary
- **Flies:** large salmon, steelhead and ocean flies, big poppers, huge bucktails for pike, and big dry flies for salmon

CLASSIC LOCH-STYLE OUTFIT – BOAT FISHING ON BIG LOCHS, LOUGHS AND LAKES

This last outfit is included as a curiosity, but the method it encompasses is a classic one that has stood the test of time.

- **Quarry:** trout, sea trout, salmon
- **Rod:** 11 or 12ft (3.3 or 3.6m) graphite rod, slow-actioned, for #5 or #6
- **Reel:** single-action or multiplying reel; backing depends on species encountered – up to 150yd (137m) for salmon
- **Fly line:** double-taper #5 floater or #6 floater for traditional-style short casting; similar # intermediate line can be useful
- **Leaders:** 12 to 20ft (3.6–6m) long with two or three droppers
- **Tippets:** 2 to 6lb (1–2.7kg)
- **Flies:** classic wet fly selection with plenty of palmered top-dropper flies; small standard Atlantic salmon and sea trout lures; tiny muddlers (for top droppers, dressed on standard wet fly 10s and smaller); range of stillwater nymphs where suitable

Putting It All Together

Not a few aspiring fly fishermen have arrived at the water's edge, raring to go, only to discover that their newly acquired and much-loved fishing tackle has no intention of allowing them to cast or even to begin to fish properly. Perhaps when they do hook a fish they find it impossible to play, a jammed reel or poor knots causing them the ultimate irritation to a novice – the loss of that all-important first trout of their fly-fishing careers.

It is not enough to have the best tackle and even to employ it brilliantly if a simple item such as a knot, or the balance of your tackle, lets you down. The importance of balanced tackle has been stressed in Chapter 1 – for good casting, balanced tackle is everything. But having acquired an immaculate rod-and-line combination and carefully not crippled it with a too-heavy reel and an understrength leader, and not having tried to use the outfit on rivers or lakes where it is too powerful, we must assemble it all. Unlike other branches of the sport of angling, the fly fisherman will benefit from spending some time at home first putting his outfit together. There are quick methods of assembling fly fishing tackle at the waterside but they are untrustworthy.

The novice may prefer to put his trust in the tried and tested knots, not the new-fangled glues and tubes, but these modern methods are worth a look.

Before we consider them we should introduce rod to reel. You may prefer to fish with your reel set up for left- or right-handed use, and the majority of reels on the market allow both functions. So decide and set the reel as necessary; it may mean turning a switch or merely moving a cog with a screwdriver. Whatever the method it is rarely a taxing job.

Depending on where you are planning to fish you will most probably want to put some backing on your reel, anything from 32 to 220yd (30–200m) as advised in Chapter 1. Wind this on under gentle tension, and distribute the line with your fingers as you wind, so that the backing forms a smooth and level basis for the fly line. Hollow backing will now be attached to the fly line by sliding the line up the backing and fixing it in place with a cynoacrilate glue. Whip over the join with fly tying silk to smooth the edge. Probably the safest knot to join flat nylon or standard monofilament line to the fly line is the needle knot. Soft backings like Terylene can be tied on with the nail knot, though it is advisable to put a single half-hitch in the fly line before tying the nail knot. Alternatively you may prefer to use glue.

It has been my experience that all cynoacrilate joins should be checked regularly because they break down very quickly in water.

Now wind on the fly line following the manufacturer's instructions. If they are lost or there were none, place the coiled fly line over a rolled-up magazine, cut any packing tyings, or untwist any wires, and unwind the line ensuring that it has no twists. These will cause unbelievable problems at a later date if they find their way on to your reel. Infuriatingly, there is no certain way of getting just enough backing and fly line to fill any particular reel at the first attempt. Again, follow the manufacturer's instructions as to capacity. Do not attempt to fish with an overfull reel, it will damage the line and make the playing of trout very difficult.

Now for the leader. As was discussed in Chapter 1, there is now a huge range of leaders available on the market, and 90 per cent of these have much to commend them. Let us discuss their attachment to the business end of the line.

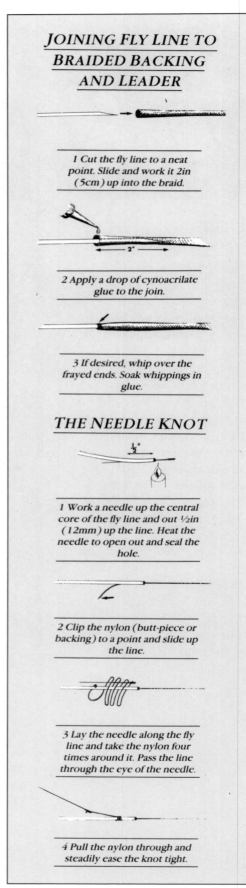

JOINING FLY LINE TO BRAIDED BACKING AND LEADER

1 Cut the fly line to a neat point. Slide and work it 2in (5cm) up into the braid.

2 Apply a drop of cynoacrilate glue to the join.

3 If desired, whip over the frayed ends. Soak whippings in glue.

THE NEEDLE KNOT

1 Work a needle up the central core of the fly line and out ½in (12mm) up the line. Heat the needle to open out and seal the hole.

2 Clip the nylon (butt-piece or backing) to a point and slide up the line.

3 Lay the needle along the fly line and take the nylon four times around it. Pass the line through the eye of the needle.

4 Pull the nylon through and steadily ease the knot tight.

THE LOOP-TO-LOOP KNOT

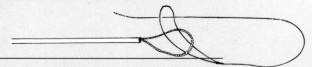

For quick and simple changes of your leader the loop-to-loop join is useful. Make a small neat loop on the end of your fly line by stripping back 1in (2.5cm) of coating from the core of the line. Double it back and sew together with fine thread (fly-tying thread is ideal), then whip over the stitching and soak well in cynoacrilate glue. The fly-line loop should be small and neat to pass through the guides (rod rings). The loop in the stiffer but slimmer nylon can be 1in (2.5cm) or more long and will actually run more smoothly through the rings than a smaller loop.

THE EMERGENCY NAIL KNOT

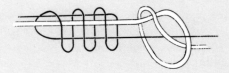

If you need to totally replace a new leader a simple overhand knot in the fly-line end will give sufficient purchase for a needle or nail knot to be tied behind it. However, it can pay to carry a needle and some matches when far from home!

SEWN AND WHIPPED LOOP ON FLY LINE

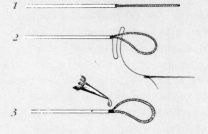

1 Strip 1in (2.5cm) of coating from the tip of the fly line.

2 Using fly-tying thread, sew the ends together to form a loop.

3 Overwhip the sewn join repeatedly and soak with cynoacrilate glue.

THE PALOMAR HITCH

1 Pass the looped nylon through the eye of the hook.

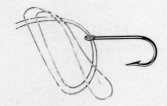

2 Tie a simple overhand knot with the loop.

3 Pass the open loop over the hook and ease the knot tight.

THE COVE KNOT

1 Lay the two lengths of nylon alongside each other.

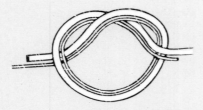

2 Make an overhand loop with both lengths.

3 Repeat four times, dampen with saliva and ease tight. One end can be left as a dropper; many anglers now favour the 'down-the-line' end, that is the one pointing away from the fly line, as the stronger option, although it may be more prone to tangling.

TUCKED BLOOD KNOT

Pass the nylon through the hook eye and twist the hook to make several turns. Take the loose end of nylon and pass it through the gap just above the hook eye. Then take the nylon back through the loop you have formed and ease the knot tight.

Generally of braided nylon, the best hollow leaders are tapered down in one length, others are joined with knots in tapered stages. Either way they are simple to attach to the fly line. The tip, which may be cut to a point, is simply threaded up inside the braid. Once there, it can be glued and overwhipped right at the end. Provided at least 16in (4cm) are slid over the fly line, a dab of glue should suffice.

To employ the useful quick-change facility of the leaders, some manufacturers offer tubes of thin plastic which lock the leaders in place, but can quickly be removed should a sinking leader be needed in place of a floater. These links are usually trustworthy, but many old hands distrust anything but a knot they have tied themselves!

Twisted leaders, the precursor of braid, are more difficult to attach neatly, and a simple loop sewn in the end of the fly line and looped to the leader is often the best method (*see* diagram).

Tapered nylon leaders can be glued inside the fly line. A hole is made by inserting a large needle 1in (2cm) or more up the core of the line then heating it to burn and seal a hole. The leader is cut to a point and slightly roughened. Cynoacrilate glue is then applied to the butt, and the leader slid up and glued inside the line. The result is a smooth join and the method can also be used to join the backing, especially shooting-head backing, to the line.

Cast connectors are tubes of smooth, strong nylon. By threading leader and line in alternate ends and knotting, they hold the two together in a sure, if rather lumpy embrace, but they do not float too well. Being the traditionalists they are, fly fishermen sometimes opt for one of two methods when joining fly line to leader which need attention away from the water. One is the needle knot, the other is the neatly sewn and whipped loop (*see* diagram). Strip the coating from 2in (5cm) of the tip of the fly line, fold it back on itself, sew it together, and whip over the join with fly-tying silk, then coat and soak the whole thing in cynoacrilate glue. Such loops at the end of the fly line are particularly useful with sunk-line tactics where leader length can be very important. They are also useful for novice casters who may opt for a length of level nylon leader and finally, the loops allow a quick change of leader, when wind and casting errors tangle it.

Many British anglers favour a permanently needle-knotted butt piece with a loop on the end, to which they then attach their required leader nylon. As has been suggested, tapered leaders are of most use on rivers, and less so with the long-leader tactics that score on stillwater, which possibly reflects the British preference for the more easily available reservoir sport. With the leader attached, the angler may want to add further lengths of nylon, either in the shape of a fine tippet, or a leader with one or more droppers, such as those necessary for the classic loch-style or various nymphing techniques.

The author has total confidence in the water knot for these droppers, and while the well-read novice will read of others he need look no further. The water knot, also known in the UK as the Cove knot, is simply tied and will produce reliable droppers (*see* diagram). If it does not, the nylon, the knot tying, or knot testing technique are at fault.

So, with line and leader indivisibly knotted, and the reel placed on the rod with the handle to the side of the angler's preference, wind the line on so that it comes through the line guard with which most reels are fitted, at the bottom of the standard fly reel. Thread the line through the rings but not, of course, through the very small keeper ring, sometimes set at right angles to the other rings and always very close to the handle.

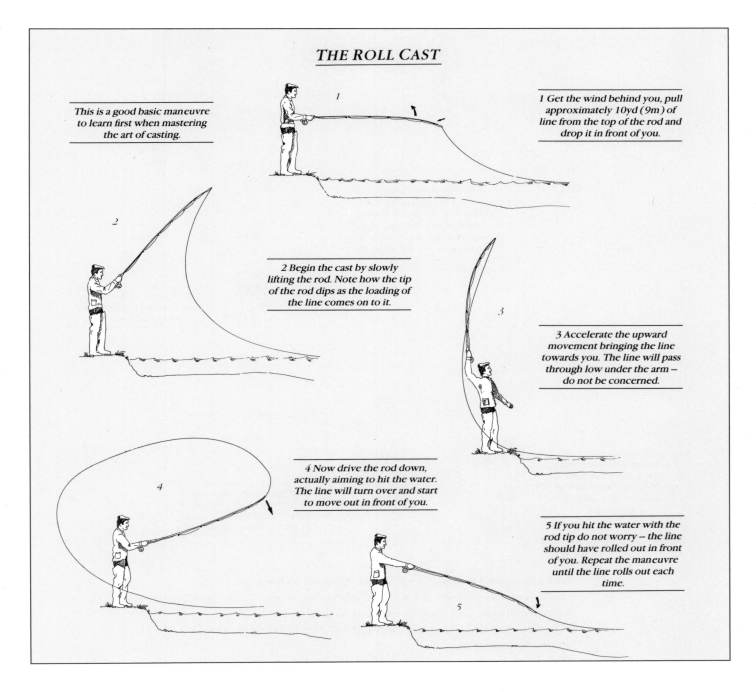

THE ROLL CAST

This is a good basic maneuvre to learn first when mastering the art of casting.

1 Get the wind behind you, pull approximately 10yd (9m) of line from the top of the rod and drop it in front of you.

2 Begin the cast by slowly lifting the rod. Note how the tip of the rod dips as the loading of the line comes on to it.

3 Accelerate the upward movement bringing the line towards you. The line will pass through low under the arm — do not be concerned.

4 Now drive the rod down, actually aiming to hit the water. The line will turn over and start to move out in front of you.

5 If you hit the water with the rod tip do not worry — the line should have rolled out in front of you. Repeat the maneuvre until the line rolls out each time.

This ring is generally far too small to be a rod ring, and when present is designed to hold the fly when the angler is on the move.

To attach the fly or flies, you have two useful choices, the blood knot for small flies, always tucked as shown, or the Palomar hitch for larger patterns, mainly lures or salmon flies (*see* diagrams). Both knots are simple to tie, and should be lubricated with saliva and gently eased-up tight. Then, like all knots, tested with a steady pressure before a fish gets a chance to ruin the day.

CASTING – SOME FIRST PRINCIPLES

The very best way to learn casting – some would say the only way – is to go to a professional tutor of repute and take a course. Sometimes it is suggested that the prospective fly fisherman should practise over dry

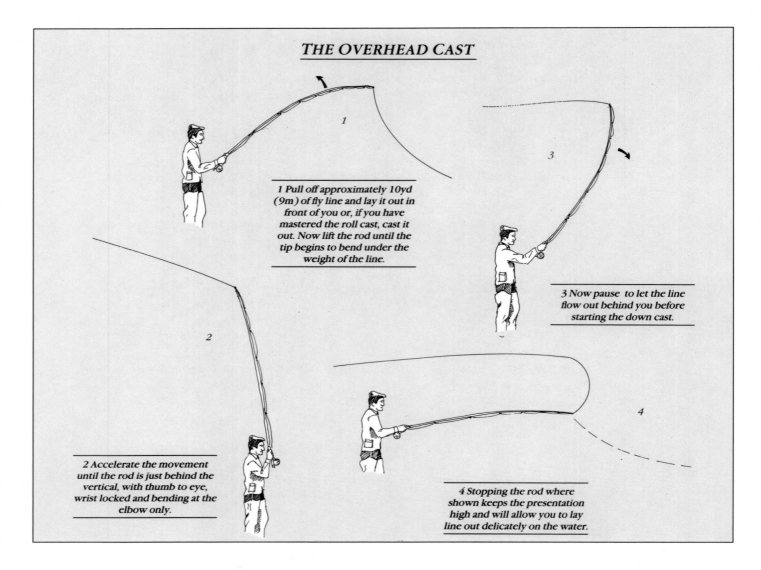

THE OVERHEAD CAST

1 Pull off approximately 10yd (9m) of fly line and lay it out in front of you or, if you have mastered the roll cast, cast it out. Now lift the rod until the tip begins to bend under the weight of the line.

3 Now pause to let the line flow out behind you before starting the down cast.

2 Accelerate the movement until the rod is just behind the vertical, with thumb to eye, wrist locked and bending at the elbow only.

4 Stopping the rod where shown keeps the presentation high and will allow you to lay line out delicately on the water.

land with a piece of wool instead of a fly. It can do no harm, but what is idiotic is to wander down to your local fishery, buy a ticket, then try to learn how to cast. That really is expensive tuition!

I will now describe the main casts and the order in which you should attempt to master them.

Roll Cast: Many leading casting instructors start their pupils off with this cast – and it makes sense. The roll cast is used where there is little space for a back cast, due to trees or high banks. The basic action is to pull enough line from the top ring to load the rod and to lay the line on the water by dropping it at your feet. Then lift the rod firmly and push it back, attempting to drive the rod top into the water. The action is staggering for the novice, but it lifts the line off the surface and drives it out over the water. It is a cast important in most casting manoeuvres, being essential to facilitate lifting off line before the actual cast. In some techniques, notably the stillwater lure and the classic loch-style, it is virtually impossible to fish properly without the ability to perform an extremely competent roll cast – and it is an easy cast.

Overhead Cast: This is the basic cast which most fly fishermen use almost all of the time. Master this cast and the rest will, or should, come easily. Follow it through the basic movements: after rolling the line off and laying it out fairly straight in front of you, raise the rod sharply to just beyond the 90 degree mark. Pause fractionally, and the line should fly out behind you. After the line has straightened behind you drive the rod forward and it should shoot out in front of you. Stop the rod at 45 degrees and the line should turn over and roll out straight in front of you. Repeat the process. The timing is all-important; insufficient line speed, or too short or too long a pause at the top of the cast, will result in hopeless casts, or tangles of the worst kind.

Single-haul Casting: If you can hold the 30ft (9m) of line (which balances your rod) in the air consistently (aerialize it), the next move is to improve your casting distance. Striving for distance – *not* accuracy – is the eternal curse of the stillwater angler who is fishing blind over large expanses of water. But long-casting skills are often necessary, and to cast further the novice will discover he must increase line speed. Hauls on the line as he casts are the way to achieve line speed. Hauls are not violent tugs, they must be properly orchestrated so that they fit into the cast in one smooth, fluid coordination of hand, arm and eye.

Start by holding the fly line in the left hand as you cast with the right. This automatically gives you the beginnings of a single haul. Now extend this grip on the line into a smooth downward haul (in the same vertical line as your rod) as you lift the flyline from the water, so accelerating the speed of the line through the air.

Now use the same smooth haul after the line has straightened out behind you – this also accelerates the line and, coupled with the correct moment of release, pushes your cast out further. A weight-forward or shooting-head line is necessary to use this cast to full effect.

Double-haul Casting: This is the standard cast for the angler who needs to reach for distance. To double haul, you perform both the motions described above – that is you accelerate the line as you lift off, then haul after it straightens out behind you to speed it forward. As in all casting, timing is more important than brute strength, and all the movements will look effortless as you watch a professional cast out a full weight-forward line.

Side Cast: To keep the line under obstructions on the back cast, or to put the fly under an obstruction on the front cast, you need to master the side cast. To achieve this you simply turn all the basic overhead casting actions on their side, with the rod horizontal or at least at an angle to the vertical. As the line will be closer to the ground or water, a good hauling technique is vital to keep the line moving fast, and to produce a tight loop.

The Loop and Casting: Every cast produces a loop in the line, behind or above the angler. This is caused when the fly line gradually unfolds behind the angler. The faster the line movement, the tighter the loop and the tighter the loop, the greater the risk of a tangle. So when double-hauling for distance on a big stillwater, with a single nymph or lure, you might manage it without tangles. You will, however, need a leader that is not too long, and you may have to avoid the dragging effect of a heavily weighted fly. When casting a team of flies, perhaps a traditional wet fly cast or a team of chironomid imitations, to haul too quickly is to invite tangles and you need to cultivate a wide, slow loop and accept some loss of casting distance.

Steeple Cast: You can also make that tight loop form a steeple above you. This is a useful cast when there are obstructions behind you, and no room to make a proper back-cast. Basically, you change the timing of the cast so that the loop forms horizontally above you, then by the timing of your forward cast, and haul, drive the line out in front. An easier alter-

THE SIDE CAST

ABOVE Side casting under an obstruction calls for the same speed, accuracy and timing as for the overhead cast, but the moves are performed on the horizontal.

native is usually the roll cast, although sometimes the small amount of line that goes behind you on this cast and the low trajectory of the line, make the cast difficult where there is confined space or vegetation under your feet.

Dealing with the Wind: Many novice casters consciously seek a bank with a nice, safe left to right wind (or vice-versa for a left-hander), or a back wind that helps to drive out their cast. They may at the same time miss the best of the sport, so it pays to have one or two tricks to overcome the wind. The way to cast into the wind is to achieve a low delivery. If you imagine that there is a 2ft (0.6m) gap below the wind, and aim your cast and delivery below that height, you will cast considerably farther than if you chose to fight the wind. When threatened with a vicious side wind which tends to blow each cast into the side of your head, the easiest way to overcome the problem is simply to turn your back on the water, and make your 'back cast' in front of you, then shoot the line back over your shoulder. This also gives you a good view of your back cast (which is now the 'actual' cast) and enables you to improve its direction and timing.

Safety: No mention of fly casting and the problem of wind would be complete without a brief reminder to always wear a hat (and possibly a turned-up collar or scarf) and sunglasses, both when fishing and practising casting. As has already been stated in the tackle section, both a hat and glasses have a role to play in helping you catch more fish as well as protecting your face and head.

Even practising with a tuft of wool in place of a fly is no defence. A high-speed fly line slapping your face is an excruciating and potentially damaging thing. Bearing that in mind, always consider bystanders and spectators when practising and watch where your back cast is going. Even the most expert fly casters forget to check this, and their victims are mainly trees. Yours might be something less resilient.

In the world of casting, first good tuition, then practice, makes perfect.

The Fly Fisherman's Fish Species

Almost every fish that swims will take a fly from time to time. And, of course, a fly can be tied to imitate a huge range of food items that will tempt them. But the fish listed in this chapter are the main quarry of the fly fisherman – plus a few personal choices, included for reasons that hopefully will become clear to the reader.

TROUT

Brown Trout *(Salmo trutta)*

To some extent the hero of our book, the brown trout is either indigenous, or stocked, all over the world. Brown is an odd description of a fish that can be as black as coal, or as silver as any salmon, depending on the season and its location. For instance the brown trout of Lough Carra in Ireland are silver blue, but about 100 miles (161km) away, on Lough Melvin, they are virtually black. *Salmo trutta* is a hardy species, surviving in some comparatively unlikely settings, needing only clean, well-oxygenated flowing water with gravel beds to spawn successfully. It will also migrate to the sea, staying close to the coast, and return up rivers and into sea lochs when it will generally be known as the sea trout.

Rainbow Trout *(Salmo gairdneri)*

This is another trout that has responded well to stocking all over the world having been introduced from the US. In a few places, in the UK and other countries, it has successfully established breeding populations. Mostly, however, away from the US, the species has relied on the fish farmer and stocking programmes for its presence. 'Rainbow' refers to the fish's bright coloration, mainly a reddish-purple banding along its side. With constant stocking in Europe, its sea-run form, the steelhead, is beginning to turn up in rivers and sea lochs in northern Europe, including the Baltic Sea, but the numbers are minute compared to the vast runs that make the steel-head a prized target on the Pacific seaboard of the US and Canada.

Cut-throat Trout *(Salmo clarki)*

Named for the vivid slash of colour at its throat, the cut-throat is common in the western US up to Alaska. This fish, too, will wander out to sea at the mouths of rivers, acquiring the bright silver of the sea trout or steelhead.

Brook Trout *(Salvelinus fontinalis)*

Known in Europe as the American brook trout, or charr (which it strictly speaking is) this is the most beautiful of the common trout in its cream and tomato-soup colours. A denizen of the eastern half of the US, the fish is being hounded out of its traditional homes by imported browns and rainbows. This species will not only do well in brooks but also exists comfortably in stillwater. Given the chance, it will also go to sea – but with the pollution of the East Coast such sea-run fish are rare these days.

The Dolly Varden *(Salvelinus malmo)*

A handsome near-relative of the brook trout, the Dolly Varden is a West Coast trout, often encountered in Alaska. Yet another occasional traveller to sea.

ABOVE Cut Throat trout.

ABOVE American Brook trout.

ABOVE Steelhead trout.

ABOVE A specimen king salmon from Lake Michigan, U.S.A.

RIGHT The king of game fish – a 27-lb (12-kg) Atlantic salmon from Norway's River Vosso.

SALMON

The Atlantic Salmon *(Salmo Salar)*

Salar, the leaper, known as the king of fish, runs from the northern Atlantic into rivers in the US and Europe and also from the North Sea into the UK, Norway and the Baltic Sea. Stocks of Atlantic salmon are now severely threatened by netting in the ocean, and by acid rain and the damming of its home rivers. The salmon is a prime fighter, given to leaps and long runs. It does not feed in freshwater and must be tempted to take a fly.

Pacific Salmon

Chinook *(Oncorhynchus tschawytscha)*

The chinook is also known as king or spring salmon, names that betray the respect in which it is held, and the time of its first runs.

The Waters We Fish

Fly fishermen owe a great deal to a handsome spotted creature known as the brown trout. Its range through the Northern hemisphere and its importation below the equator, meant that the most interesting and challenging fish the fly fisherman seeks is widely available. Not the least reason for this is the trout's remarkable ability to feed, breed and reproduce in almost any clean stillwater with some sort of feeder stream, or in a wide range of rivers and streams from the smallest to the largest.

Most of the other game fish will be found in similar locations. The various migratory species, the salmon, steelhead and sea trout require access to the sea – but river-fed lakes and lochs will have their runs. If the waters worth the fly fisherman's attention are varied, so are the locations where his quarry may be found. Only local knowledge will answer some of the questions posed at various locations, but several things are certain. Fish will be found where they may stay in safety, where there is an adequate supply of food and where they may expend the minimum energy. There are exceptions to these general rules, and they will mainly exist when fish find their actions governed by spawning urges.

Where 'aggression' replaces a natural feeding urge, behaviour patterns can change and this is the greatest fascination in pursuing the Atlantic salmon. But bearing in mind the basic rules, consider the fly fisherman's many venues, and where his fly may most effectively be cast.

ABOVE Delightful and enchanting surroundings add an air of mystery to this creek in North Carolina.

ABOVE Streamy water of this sort fishes best for trout in times of drought – otherwise small fish may be your reward.

OPPOSITE LEFT A powerfully flowing but deep river offers many problems for the fly fisherman.

OPPOSITE RIGHT Idaho's Salmon River, famed home for the migratory rainbow trout, the steelhead.

SMALL STREAMS

These may be alkaline and rich in food or sparse and acid. Generally the anglers' target will be brown trout, brook trout, rainbows and grayling, and in various venues they will range up to several pounds or kilos. Such fish will always be challenging, and the best fish will hold in the most protected lies, where food comes easily. To do this, fish will see off all smaller interlopers, even eating them. In the sparser streams, generally in hill or mountain country, there will be very few specimen trout compared with hundreds of smaller ones. They get larger by finding the best lies, and they should be sought in the deeper holes, below undercut banks, wherever fallen trees or boulders create snags, and wherever a quirk of the current collects food in a steady stream.

The experienced angler will consider such areas, discovering which method will best present his fly to the fish. It might be a large dry fly, plopped heavily over the lie, a heavily loaded nymph dunked into the fish's lair, or a lure or small fish imitation swum enticingly by. Long casts or heavy tackle are rarely necessary on the jump-across streams. What is necessary is the belly-to-the ground commando-style approach; and an almost second-sighted ability to sniff out the lie of a better fish. No prizes are given for standing on the skyline or thrashing the water to foam with a bad cast. Mastery of the underwater currents is useful too; once it is in the water, getting the fly down, across, or under to a trout can be very difficult. This is no place for petty restrictions of upstream or downstream – the fly must be flicked, catapulted, or twitched into place.

TROUT LIES ON THE RIVER

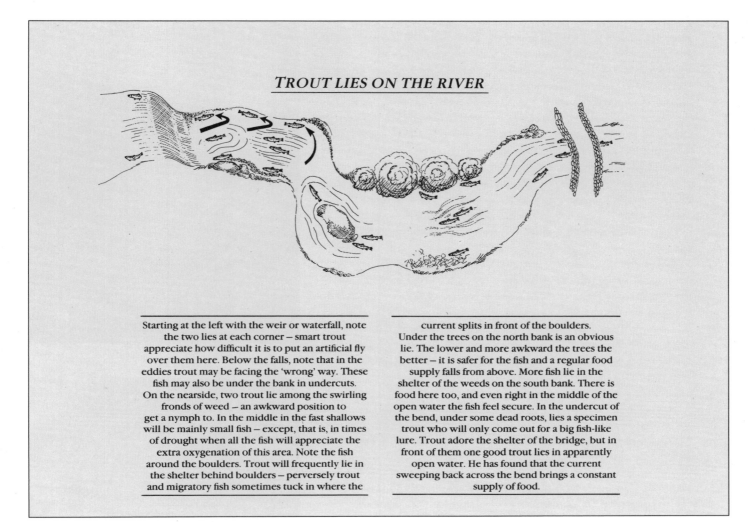

Starting at the left with the weir or waterfall, note the two lies at each corner – smart trout appreciate how difficult it is to put an artificial fly over them here. Below the falls, note that in the eddies trout may be facing the 'wrong' way. These fish may also be under the bank in undercuts. On the nearside, two trout lie among the swirling fronds of weed – an awkward position to get a nymph to. In the middle in the fast shallows will be mainly small fish – except, that is, in times of drought when all the fish will appreciate the extra oxygenation of this area. Note the fish around the boulders. Trout will frequently lie in the shelter behind boulders – perversely trout and migratory fish sometimes tuck in where the current splits in front of the boulders.

Under the trees on the north bank is an obvious lie. The lower and more awkward the trees the better – it is safer for the fish and a regular food supply falls from above. More fish lie in the shelter of the weeds on the south bank. There is food here too, and even right in the middle of the open water the fish feel secure. In the undercut of the bend, under some dead roots, lies a specimen trout who will only come out for a big fish-like lure. Trout adore the shelter of the bridge, but in front of them one good trout lies in apparently open water. He has found that the current sweeping back across the bend brings a constant supply of food.

MEDIUM-SIZED RIVERS

Here our quarry may be any one of the game fish, and the nature of the stream can be infinitely variable – from the lush green of the Test or Itchen in Hampshire's green chalk-stream meadow land, to the rugged rocks of the Snake or Rogue rivers in the western US; from the acid upland salmon rivers such as the Airey of south-west Scotland, racing to the sea in a few miles of spate river, to the steady trundle of dredged and canalized middle sections of rivers everywhere, featureless and dull but often full of trout. Somewhere in this group you can place most of the classic trout streams of the world and quite a few of the best rivers for migratory species. With the salmon, sea trout and steelhead there are infinite possibilities, and only local knowledge will clearly mark all the lies and runs that the fish will occupy. But a trout is a trout, and it will pay to consider a number of natural features that will always attract the fish.

Under some conditions – low water, extreme warmth, slight pollution deoxygenating the water, extremely clear water – you may find trout in the fast streamy runs provided there is sufficient depth. Certainly you will find small trout, grayling, and salmon parr in the streamy sections and they will be easily caught. For the better trout, however, look for areas where the current divides, around a rock, or other obstruction, or splits, leaving slack areas, eddies, undercuts or deep boiling pot-holes. Fish these areas with care, avoiding extremely deep slow water, or canal-like sections which often seem devoid of trout.

Manmade features are to be found on many of these waters; bridges shelter fish – often the uncatchable giants – and change the flow where their standings push aside the current. Likewise groynes pushing out into the flow, weirs and other obstructions such as waterfalls, cut their own deep pools and radically change the speed and nature of a river. Man may also be responsible for the bankside trees and bushes which can overhang the water, collecting weed and food and sheltering trout.

Inch worms, beetles and other insects fall from this vegetation to feed the sheltering fish.

Where the undermining force of the river becomes too much, a tree may topple into the river, again attracting and sheltering fish, and providing a nightmare of snags for the unwary angler. Rocks in the river also affect the flow and shelter fish, sometimes in the deflection of water upstream but more often below. A wide range of casts will be needed to reach these fish, to cover the water, and to fish the fly properly.

LARGE RIVERS

Chasing the salmon and other migratory fish of these waters has its own problems, and the long European fly rods of up to 18ft (5.5m) or more, with heavy double-taper lines, were often seen as the solution. Now even on the most traditional of Scottish rivers there is the beginning of a change, already taken place elsewhere, to an outfit such as the standard heavy fly-fishing outfit described in Chapter 1, with shooting heads and plenty of backing. But wading the classic large rivers such as the Tweed or Spey with chest waders and a long fly rod is an art in itself.

All that is true of the other bodies of running water is true of the large rivers. Mentally break them down into smaller streams, put on the waders, and get out to positions that allow you to properly fish your fly through what looks like a recognizable lie – it may be a huge boulder sheltering a salmon, a situation which, in miniature, you have observed before on a tiny mountain trout stream.

TOP The River Test might well be a rainbow-infested shadow of its former self, but it is still the world's most famous chalk stream.

ABOVE And the Itchen is still the second most famous – both rise in the chalk downs of Hampshire in southern England.

OPPOSITE The Helmsdale River, Sutherland, Scotland is a spate river where conditions of recent rain are vital to salmon catching success.

ABOVE Some stretches of
Scotland's mighty river Spey
need long-casting to cover the
salmon lies.

RIGHT The Yellowstone river.

STILLWATERS

Waters of this kind do not always run deep, and trout may be taken in shallow pools, stocked or unstocked, less than 10ft (3m) deep – shallower still if the owner or manager is around to protect his stock and keep the predators away. Shallow, clear pools of under 10 acres (4 hectares) are best treated like a river. Trout in a stillwater environment are more inclined to cruise about than the river-borne fish. A wide, steady river pool may hold cruising, feeding trout moving on top; a stillwater will invariably have some cruising fish, especially if rainbows are among the stock.

I remember one pool where all the rainbows cruised in open, if weeded, water, while the browns stayed close under marginal trees, rising to terrestrial insects falling in. I took a limit of fish nymphing with a Woolly Worm pattern. Dried out and cast as a dry fly, it took a fine brown that had risen persistently under a bankside tree. Much of the sport with these cruising fish is visual. They must be picked off as they cruise past, and often you get but one chance. Presentation and cast must be perfect right down to the sinking speed of your fly.

Otherwise, on the small clear waters look for features similar to those found in rivers that hold trout – especially any weedbeds. Small, coloured stillwaters are better prospected with a bright lure or wet fly initially. Eventually they may offer superb sport to nymph or even dry fly, but trout in coloured water provide an unnatural situation, one in which they may become just bottom grubbers.

RESERVOIRS – THE EUROPEAN STANDBY

The thriving British stillwater trouting scene – indeed the whole British trouting scene – relies greatly on a series of heavily stocked water-supply reservoirs. One at least, Rutland Water, approaches the delights and problems of a wild fishery in its size and complexity. Here, trout get time

TOP Norway, where many rivers have been devastated by acid rain.

ABOVE Norway, where sea and freshwater meet in huge fjords and rivers.

LEFT Secure in the knowledge he has the necessary equipment to hand, nothing need disturb the angler's concentration.

WHERE TO FISH ON STILLWATER

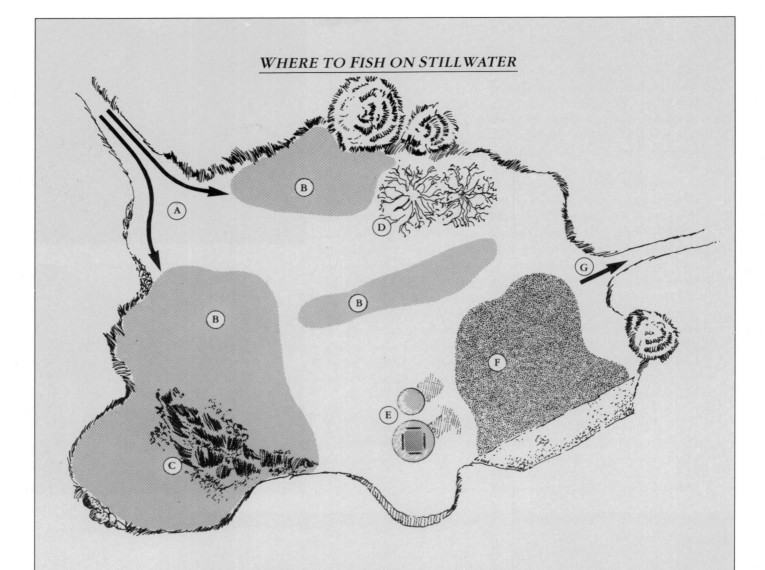

This imaginary map gives you the clues:

A The entry of a river or stream. Late or early in the season, this will hold post- or pre-spawning trout. In warm periods the water will be more oxygenated here and trout may gather to take advantage. When the stream is in flood it will bring both food and possibly quantities of silt into the lake. Trout are very partial to earthworms, but less keen on being blinded by muddy water.

B These areas are shallows. You may well take fish from the bank over these areas early and late in the day – fish will move onto the shallows to feed at night. However, the central shallow area may well be a boat fishing hotspot, especially when worked over-the-front, loch style.

C This is an area of weedbeds. This will be particularly attractive to the fish that move in to feed at dusk, and will probably hold some trout all day. It will be good too in the early season when last year's dead weeds will hold what remains of the food supply.

D These dead trees or sticks in the water will be a hotspot at fry-feeding time. Here the little prey fish will try to shelter (as they will in the weedbeds) and the trout will seek them out. The sticks may also shelter newly stocked trout.

E This area will also shelter prey fish, and being over deeper water will attract some of the better fish. This is a tower or other structure and there may well be underwater pipes or aerators near it, all of which attract fish.

F This is an area of deeper water. Here big lures and fast-sinking lines may take some better fish. This area has been artificially deepened by the building of a dam. The corners of the dam will always hold fish, particularly stocked trout, and fishing anywhere along the dam wall with a fast-sinker and a bouyant fly may produce specimen trout.

G This is the river's exit. If this is a loch or lough with access to the sea, this may be the hotspot to intercept migratory trout and salmon.

to grow on and become somewhat feral. Other, more circular waters give their fish less chance of escape, and consequently have a high turnover of stock. Stock-pen fed trout can be easy targets because these fish know man as the provider of food, not as a predator. Few of these waters manage any degree of recruitment among their trout stocks. Some browns breed in their feeder streams, and the occasional rainbow parr appears on some waters, but angling pressure and the natural order demands heavy stocking. Similar waters are to be found world-wide, and there is a rapidly growing interest in this style of sport in France. But it is mainly in the UK where the vast majority of these waters remain fly only.

Reservoir trouting has led to the invention of a number of borderline fly-fishing techniques in many ways more akin to trolling and spinning, but worthy of interest for the success they have enjoyed with deep-lying trout over the past two decades. Otherwise this fishing is full of variety, with a huge range of tactics producing trout of varying degrees of quality. In the rich English Midland reservoirs – Grafham, Eye Brook, Rutland – trout will feed naturally a week or so after stocking, and sometimes treble their weight in a season, particularly the fast growing rainbows. With a hundred years of high-quality sport behind it, the British stillwater scene must be taken seriously. The world-wide fly fishing scene already owes it a debt for evolving new styles, methods and flies.

ABOVE Fishing at dawn on Europe's largest manmade stillwater, Rutland Water, a reservoir in Leicestershire, England. The target fish were large end-of-season brown trout. Stocked as fingerlings, they now reach 14lb (6kg) or more.

LARGER NATURAL LAKES, LOCHS AND LOUGHS

All over the world there are naturally stocked, high-quality trout lakes, each with their own strains of trout. Some of them support mixed populations of game fish, especially where there is access to a major river or better still the sea. Consider Lough Melvin on the borders of Eire and Ulster. Here there are four genetically different strains of *Salmo trutta* – browns, ferox and the delightfully named sonneghan and gillaroo, salmon and, in the depths, charr. Though the lough is acid, and low on food, for some reason there are no sea trout – the browns never migrate to sea.

Fishing such waters is a delight, the classic British loch-style, as it is known, is as likely to draw up and hook a 9oz (255g) brown as a 9lb (4kg) salmon – I know, I've done both on one day. The historical richness of the great Irish loughs – Corrib, Conn, Mask, and the great Scottish lochs – Leven, Watten, or Orkney's Harray, has a charm irrelevant to fishing, which enhances it even more. Here, some of the great international fly patterns saw their birth, flies which though tied for one species do great slaughter of another 3,000 miles (4,800km) away. Old boats and old boatmen still ply these waters, and though the modern skills and styles of fly fishing may eventually revolutionize the sport on such waters, change will be long and slow.

STILLWATER FISHING: FINDING THE FISH

'Stillwater' is a misnomer. It is in fact never still, whether the movement comes from pressure and temperature change, wind, or the action of feeder streams. Underwater currents are as significant to trout as more visible river currents are. They will push food around, and trout are lazy enough to wait for its arrival at their noses. Cruising fish will generally move upwind, even at depth. More static populations of trout can be sought around structures, natural or manmade. Dam walls seem to have a universal appeal to all trout in most conditions and seasons.

Towers, piers and structures that shelter small fish will bring the predatory trout in. Feeder streams will often attract trout late and early in their season, usually drawn by spawning urges, sometimes to feed on the roe and young of other spawners.

Weedbeds are worthy of attention, and even on the largest stillwater, odd natural features sometimes cause fish to tarry. A salmon moving into a sea loch on its way to the spawning grounds may pause by the end of a stone wall or fence – there is no apparent logic but it happens too often to be coincidence.

Generally, on the very large waters, a ghillie, boatman, or guide is a safe investment. Even on the homely lowland waters of England, some employ boatmen; on the vastness of a Scottish loch, Irish lough or the huge North American lakes, there is also the safety factor to consider. Much of the best trout fishing water on any huge lake is shallow. On some, huge fish may be taken in quite shallow water. On many waters, sharp sub-surface rocks are always a threat in the best fishing areas.

Fly fishing tactics are not really applicable to the very big deep-water lake trout, or the British ferox. There are deep fishing methods, but they lack finesse. Never neglect shallow water surrounded by deeps (what the Irish logically call a sunken island), for it will hold your best stillwater chance of finding big fish that will take your fly.

To sum up, think trout on all waters. Think lazy fish which prefer the current to bring the food. Think safety, shelter, and a pecking order that means the best spots, often the most difficult to fish, invariably hold the best fish. And having considered all that, your fish of a lifetime from a stillwater will probably come from nowhere in a blur over an unconsidered spot. May that fish not depart as quickly when your time comes.

TOP Worldwide contrasts: master British nymph angler Gordon Fraser plays a rainbow on a small put-and-take water in Northamptonshire, England but Ringstead Grange's few acres would be swallowed thousands of times in this Arkansas reservoir, home of many game fish species ABOVE

OPPOSITE These beautiful stillwater rainbows have fine tails and fins.

Fly Tying

My aim in writing this introduction to the art of fly tying is to put together the elements of the way in which I have taught fly tying to a great many people over the past 20 years and to provide the basis for many more to join the ranks of those who make flies. Men, women, youngsters and the retired and yes, even those with disabilities can all tie flies and find magic in creating a thing of beauty from scraps of feather, fur, thread and tinsel wrapped round a hook.

I have heard many reasons given to explain the desire to tie flies. They include the pure practicalities of wanting to make variations on commercially available patterns so as to achieve a better catch rate; the wish to save money by making one's own; as a way of combining an interesting hobby for the dark evenings with the sport of fly fishing; even to the ambition to tie a perfect fly just as an art form involving intricate hand manipulations.

Every person who makes flies can pitch their skills at any level of proficiency they wish but we all have to start with the basics and this book will set the reader off on the right course: after that it is up to you to decide how far to take it.

OPPOSITE Rainbow perfection, Peter Cockwill with an 18lb 14oz trophy.

BELOW Peter Cockwill with a 20lb 7oz rainbow caught at Avington in Hampshire in 1986.

Fly tying may appear an immensely complex and highly skilled subject when first witnessed at, say a State Fair or Country Show and I have often heard someone say: 'I would never be able to do such a thing, my hands are too clumsy' or that their eyes were not good enough. I will repeat that anyone who wants to and is taught properly can make flies and I know of men whose work involves the hardest manual labour and whose hands are stiff and badly cracked and yet who make the most exquisite flies and I have taught people with poor eyesight, and those who can barely peel a potato, to make flies which catch fish; the ultimate test of an artificial fly.

One thing for sure, you will always remember the first fish you catch on a fly of your own tying. Large or small, it matters not for the important thing is that the fish saw your fly as an edible item and took it. My first attempts at fly tying were without the aid of a book or any form of instruction and the resultant 'fly' was a bit of a mess but it caught me a trout from a little creek and now, 30 years later, I can still see that flash of gold as the 10in brownie darted up from the gravel and seized my fly and made my day.

Since that day I have caught many thousands of fish on my own flies, including bluegills in an Oregon desert lake, steelheads in a Washington stream, king salmon in Alaska, brown trout from Ireland and a memorable fish indeed, the once British record rainbow trout at 20lb 7oz from Avington Lakes, Hants, but since overtaken by a 21lb 4oz fish from Loch Argyll, Scotland.

Fly tying has let me sit at a fly-tying bench alongside such greats as John Veniard and Taff Price and to fish with the legendary Lee Wulff in Africa and Jim Teeny in Oregon, as well as providing many exhilarating experiences beside river and lake which have led to lasting friendships and all with the common bond of the fly tyer.

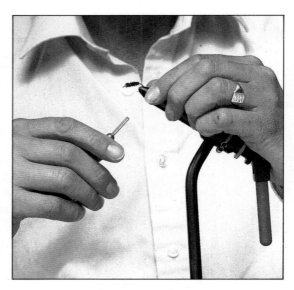

ABOVE The ideal working position, with the fly held firmly in the vice.

WHAT IS A FLY?

To a fisherman the art of fly tying embraces not only the representation of actual flies but also a much wider spectrum in that imitations of all manner of aquatic life can be created, including shrimps, small fish, snails and frogs. In fact, anything that a fish might eat can be suggested by the tying of an artificial fly. There are patterns that do not actually represent any living creature but nevertheless they catch fish and because they are created at the fly-tying vice they are called artificial flies.

An understanding of the main groupings of artificial flies will help to make sense of the many patterns in this book and the reasons for their construction. I divide flies into four principal groups, with the first being the nymphs.

NYMPHS

Under this group come all the aquatic stages of the many flies which hatch from water and creatures which spend their entire lives underwater, such as the shrimps, hoglouse (cress sows) and water beetles. Flies tied to represent this group are mostly imitative.

DRY FLIES

This group includes all the adult insects which emerge from the nymphal stages as well as terrestrial flies which find their way on to water and other land or tree-based insects which fall on to the surface. Again, flies tied to represent this group are mostly imitative although some can be said to be suggestive in that their tying does not imitate the fly but merely suggests it when seen by a fish below the surface.

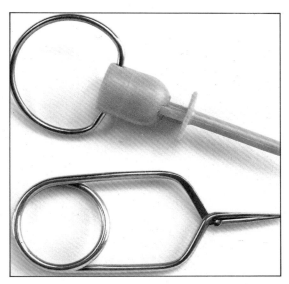

ABOVE Traditional and
Eezi hackle pliers.

STANDARD WETS

These are the flies which in reality imitate very little and as their name implies are fished under the surface. They are mostly very old patterns which follow a basically similar format using a wide range of materials, and certainly represent something to the fish but what that is is not clear. But wet flies do catch fish and because they are a challenge to tie well they are essential work for a fly tyer.

LURES

These often represent nothing that swims or lives near water because of their size and colour but they also include patterns tied to represent fish, mice, frogs and other creatures which fish eat from time to time. Many lures are often nothing more than larger versions of standard wets. Fish do take lures but whether from territorial or sexual aggression or because they look and act 'edible' we will never know. Suffice to say that fish do take lures. Why a feeding fish that will steadfastly refuse the most carefully tied and fished imitation of the creatures it is feeding on will hurl itself at a large, gaudy lure is a mystery. Virtually all artificial flies fall within these four groups and the techniques shown in this book will enable flies from all of them to be tied.

The Essentials

There are some tools which are necessary for fly tying and it is well to become familiar with them from the beginning. At the end of the book I have listed a few additional tools but to begin with there are some that are needed to form the basis of your kit.

THE VICE

The hook has to be held firmly in order to make the operations of fly tying as simple as possible and the easiest way of doing this is by the use of a purpose-made vice. It is true that some fly tyers hold the hook in their fingers but I would never presume to teach anyone in that manner as it unnecessarily complicates matters. Fly-tying vices range from the cheap and nasty to wonderful precision tools, but what we require is a functional tool that holds the hook firmly and is not too expensive. For about £10 there are some super vices imported from southern Asia which are more than adequate, and are marketed by a variety of tackle outlets. They are essentially of two types which have collet-type jaws operated by a screw or a metal lever on a cam.

A collet is a tapered and divided piece of metal which when drawn backwards through a tube causes the ends to be compressed together so that objects can be gripped. A fly-tying vice is made so that the collet ends come together as level jaws to grip the hook securely. Personally I think that the most straightforward system of tightening the collet jaws is with a screw operation as this is more positive than the lever and easier to set. Later, you may find a lever vice to be faster and more efficient.

The shaft of the vice goes into a clamp which can be fixed to a table-top and it is as well to choose a suitable work area where either good natural light falls on to the vice or a suitable artificial light source can be positioned. It is best to have the light coming from above and behind on to the work area. I assume throughout this book that the instructions are for right-handed persons but where applicable I have included special instructions for the left-handed.

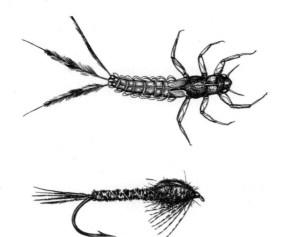

An Ephemerid nymph and a standard imitation.

An adult Ephemerid and a split wing dry fly.

Positioning the vice for ease of operation is largely a matter of adjustment to your own personal posture but generally it is best to have the vice just below eye-level when at a seated position and about 10in in front of your body.

SCISSORS

After the vice – some would say before it – the next most important piece of equipment is a really good pair of scissors. Fly tying involves cutting fine materials with a good degree of accuracy and this just cannot be achieved with scissors which are either blunt or which have tips that do not meet properly. Invest in as good a pair as you can afford and look after them by using them to cut fine materials only, NEVER wire or tinsel. It is far better to have another, cheap pair for cutting metal or coarse material. Get into the habit right away of having two pairs and using each for its correct purpose.

The choice of whether to have the scissors with a curve to the tips is yours but do make sure that the tool is not too long, 4 to 6in is about right, and that it is comfortable to use in that the finger holes are big enough and the cutting operation is not stiff. Check before you buy scissors by asking to cut a single feather fibre with the very tip of the blades. You should be able to do so with the absolute minimum of effort.

HACKLE PLIERS

This is a simple little device which operates like a miniature pair of fixed-jaw pliers to grip small and delicate materials. Mostly used to grip hackles, hackle pliers are a very useful tool and there are several different designs. The conventional type has stood the test of time although I like the Eezi model where a plunger action allows a small piece of wire to grip the hackle. Relatively inexpensive, £1 or so, but an essential tool.

WHIP-FINISH TOOL

At first sight this looks like one of those fiendishly cunning devices for making a complete idiot out of a beginner. But a well-made fly should be completed with a whip finish to give it strength and although this is possible to produce by hand the whip finish is easy when done with this remarkable tool.

These are all you need in the way of tools to make fly tying as straightforward as possible and when we move on to techniques you will see where each has its place and function. I prefer to keep my tools in a leather wallet where they are safe and always to hand, especially as I do not have the luxury of a permanent fly-tying bench.

BOBBIN HOLDER

Consider that the whole essence of fly tying involves using a fine thread to tie materials to the hook and you can understand that anything which helps to control accurate placement of the thread will be of enormous benefit. What a bobbin holder does is to grip the spool so that it will only release more thread when just enough of a pull is made to allow the spool to revolve. When allowed to hang from the hook the weight of the holder and the grip of its arms should prevent the spool from turning so that effectively the bobbin holder acts as a tension control for the thread. Also, being fed through a fine tube, the thread can be very accurately placed and if you get into the habit of holding the bobbin in the palm of your hand the tube becomes an extension of your fingers.

There are several different designs of bobbin holder so choose one that you like and which feels comfortable. Problems can occur when a sharp bit inside the tube-lip cuts the thread but the latest type have a ceramic liner which never wears and does not develop a cutting edge. I have used the simple metal ones for years and got through many spools of thread with no problem.

DUBBING NEEDLE

Quite simply a needle set in a handle and apart from its main use of picking out dubbed material bodies it has a host of other uses in fly tying. A dubbing needle will cost less than a pair of hackle pliers, or you can make your own.

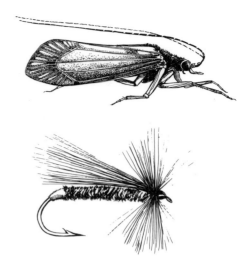

A typical Caddis fly and the fly tyer's imitation.

Proportions

The most common theme in my method of teaching fly tying is continually to emphasise the need to get the dressing of a fly put together in the correct proportions, by which is meant the relative length of, say, the hackle and tail to the size of hook being used and the insect or creature being imitated. It is true that greatly exaggerating the size of one portion of a fly will sometimes enhance its attractiveness to a fish but usually it is better to keep all the elements of the dressing in proportion.

Referring again to the four principal groups of flies it is fairly easy to prepare a representative diagram of each and indicate the correct proportions.

Starting off with group 1, the nymphs, this is a diagram of a typical nymph dressing. It is shown alongside a drawing of a natural Ephemerid nymph and I hope that you see the similarity. Of course, the copy does not resemble the real insect but the proportions are right:

(a) The natural insect has a segmented abdomen, almost always seven segments, and the artificial should suggest this with its ribbing of the abdomen.

(b) The natural has its abdomen about twice as long as the thorax – look at the artificial!

(c) The natural has a tail roughly the length of the abdomen and its legs are also the same length. The fibres we use to suggest the tail and legs therefore need to be in proportion.

(d) The natural has a distinct hump to its thorax, this is where the embryo wings are housed. Our imitation has the same pronounced hump.

Moving on to group 2, I have shown a typical upwing adult Ephemerid against the fly tyer's suggestion and a roof-winged Caddis fly against its artificial. Look at the segmentation, length of wings, angle of wings, thickness of body and length of legs, and the absence or presence of tail. All are in proportion to the natural creature.

Group 3 is slightly more difficult to explain because here we are not imitating any specific form of life but suggesting by virtue of colour and form that the artificial we have created appears edible. There are, however, certain ground-rules with regard to proportions on standard wets that if adhered to will make the fly not only very attractive to look at from our human, aesthetic point of view but also appealing to the fish.

Standard Wet Dry Dressings. Invicta and Butcher.

The diagram shows two typical standard wet fly dressings. Notice how certain elements of the artificial are kept in proportion to a natural insect even though this type of fly rarely actually imitates one. The ribbing of the abdomen again shows seven segments. The tail, wing and hackle

A typical hair-wing lure.

Matuka style.

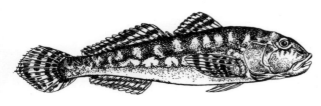

Don Gapen's original
Muddler Minnow and the fish
it suggests.

A leech or nobbler type of
lure.

lengths are relative to a natural, so once again we are working on correct proportions. Finally, to group 4, the lures.

Most flies in this category represent nothing but, as has been said earlier, they are often little more than enlarged standard wets and again therefore the same standards of proportion apply. Look at the drawing of a typical hair-wing lure and you can see immediately the same proportioning as the standard wet.

A streamer pattern or Matuka follows much the same idea but enlarges one element, in this case the wing length.

A Muddler originally intended to imitate a minnow (in Europe Phoxinus; in the US a number of small baitfish), so a drawing of the Muddler and the original minnow shows just how far away from the original theme some Muddler patterns now are. And they all of them catch fish!

Lures with mobile tails, called leeches in the US, and nobblers in the UK, rely on a very long tail of soft material, either manmade or natural, to give the lure a wriggling, pulsating movement when retrieved. A brilliant imitation of a black leech, but what does a magenta pattern suggest? Goodness knows, but at times the fish will impale themselves on it. Even a wiggle-tail fly has to have the correct proportions or it will not work properly when retrieved. A 2in tail pulses; a 4in one wiggles. When we move on to actual techniques I shall continually refer to the need to get the correct proportions, so read back over this section. It is very important.

HOOKS

Without a hook we have little chance of catching a fish and there are now hundreds of different hook patterns all based on a pointed, bent and barbed length of wire. Modern fly tying is done with an eyed hook either straight, up or down-eyed depending on personal preference for the type of fly being tied. The length of the shank can vary tremendously as can the gape of the hook and the set of the point. Hooks come either plain or forged, the latter having the bend compressed to give it more strength. The modern trend in fly fishing is to use barbless hooks so that an unwanted fish can be released with the minimum injury and so provide future sport. However, the vast majority of fly hooks are barbed and a range of commonly used patterns is shown.

Hooks are tempered in that the metal is heat-treated to harden it, but tempering is an absolute science for the hook must not be so brittle that it breaks when under tension, ie when in the mouth of a fish, and nor must it be so soft that it straightens out under a pull.

If as a fly tyer you are going to spend a considerable amount of time constructing a fly on a hook then the first thing you should do is to test its temper. If you do not, then your own temper is likely to be very severely tested if after much effort and time the hook breaks or straightens on the first fish it hooks. However, testing a hook takes but a moment and you do it as soon as the hook is placed in the vice.

At this point you will learn how to place a hook correctly into a fly-tying vice. The object is to cover the point of the hook with the jaws of the vice so that the tying thread does not catch on the sharp point and cut it. The hook must also be held so that the shank is level to make the tying operation easier and you do this by getting a good hold with the vice jaws on the lower part of the bend. Do not screw up the vice jaws so tight that the face of the jaws can be damaged, use just enough grip to ensure that the hook is firmly held.

The temper-testing operation is not too technical, all you do is to depress the hook end with your thumb and let it go. If the hook bends or breaks discard it and try another. Ideally, it should return instantly to its original shape with a 'ping'.

The old adage that you get the best by paying the most applies very much to hooks but even then you will get the occasional bad one in a batch.

Fly tyers have an enormous range of patterns from which to choose and there is a pattern for every conceivable fly within the different patterns made by Eagle Claw of the US, Mustad of Norway and Partridge of England.

To start fly tying I suggest that you obtain a packet of 25 each of the following hooks:

Size 12 Sproat bend standard-length shank, down eye.
Size 10 Limerick bend standard-shank.length, down eye.
Size 12 Sproat bend standard-shank length, up eye.
Size 10 Perfect bend long-shank, down eye.

With this selection you can tie nymphs, dry flies, standard wets and lures and then, later on, you can make other flies on patterns of your own selection or based on the recommendation of the tyer who originated the fly you want to make.

Look after your hooks by keeping them dry: corrosion is a terrible thing for fishing hooks and has been the cause of many a lost fish. A small compartmented plastic box makes an ideal storage container, with the advantage that the hook types are readily seen. Make sure that the lid fits securely, for one day you will drop your hook box and it is not much fun picking them out of the carpet and sorting out several hundred different hooks into sizes and patterns. It teaches you all about hooks, but what a way to learn!

With a little knowledge of hooks and one of a suitable temper in the vice now is the time to move to the first proper stage of becoming a fly tyer.

ABOVE The correct position of a hook in the vice.

Techniques

Here comes the difficult stuff! How do you get all those little bits of feather, thread and tinsel on to a half-inch-long hook and make it look like a fly worth putting on the end of your line? Remember what Taff Price said in his Foreword about his first flies being absolutely dreadful and how I said the same thing in the Introduction about my own early efforts?

You now have the benefit of both mine and Taff's experience and the fact that we have tied many thousands of flies and taught each other – and a great many other people – how to share this super hobby of fly tying.

Take a Size 10 standard-shank hook and put it in the vice. We are going to learn how to start and finish the fly before any material is applied to the hook.

Most books on fly tying tell you to lay the thread on to the hook shank in touching turns from the eye to the bend. However, other than for very fine tying I have never believed in doing this and all I want to teach you is how to make flies to fish with. If you want to go on to perfection of technique later on then that is the subject of another book. Now we are going to tie flies.

With the bobbin held in the right hand and about 4in of thread protruding from the bobbin, take hold of the end of the thread with the left hand and place your hand at the lower axis of the vice as shown in the photographs.

Lay the thread on to the hook shank roughly midway and take four even turns round the shank, going away from the body and working towards the hook eye.

Stop and then take four more turns going back down towards the bend so that you cover the previous four turns. Now you can let go of the thread in the left hand and allow the bobbin to hang down below the hook and the thread will stay in place. That's it, the first stage is over: you have the thread on the hook.

Next, take the thread down towards the bend and back up towards the eye, not necessarily to form a base for the dressing but more to get the hang of holding the bobbin and using the end of the tube as though it is your fingers to get very accurate placement of the thread. Take off the thread and do the whole thing again and end up with the bobbin hanging off the hook just down from the eye.

Cut off the waste end and run the tying thread up to the hook eye. Having started the fly we are now going to finish it. It might seem odd but the hardest thing you will learn is how to finish a fly properly. It is no good having got to the stage of completing the dressing of a fly and then finding out that you do not know how to finish it off! Learn the whip finish technique and you will have no further problems with fly tying. There are two ways of doing a whip finish, one is with your hands and the other is with a tool. At first, both seem impossible but if you follow these instructions and refer constantly to the photographs you will have no problems.

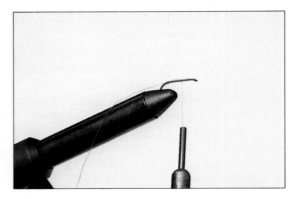

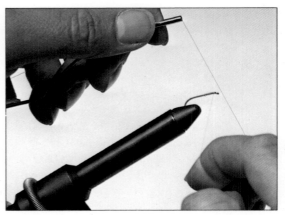

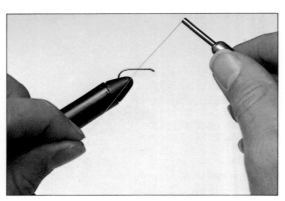

LEFT Tying thread crossed over the shank.

BELOW LEFT Four turns of thread towards the eye.

TOP RIGHT Four turns back to the bend and the thread is attached.

ABOVE RIGHT Hand whip finish.

RIGHT With a clockwise rotation of your hand and using the forefinger as a lead you trap the thread from the bobbin against the hook shank with the loop in your fingers.

BELOW RIGHT Still using the forefinger to maintain loop tension, the other two fingers now press on to the bark thread of the loop so as to turn the thread around the shank.

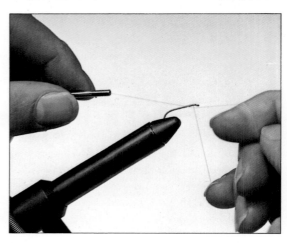

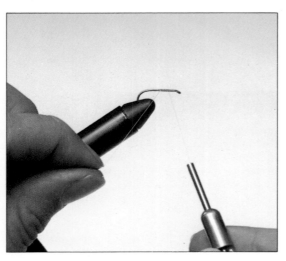

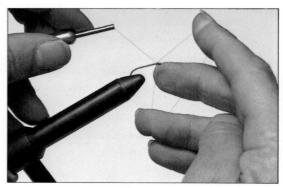

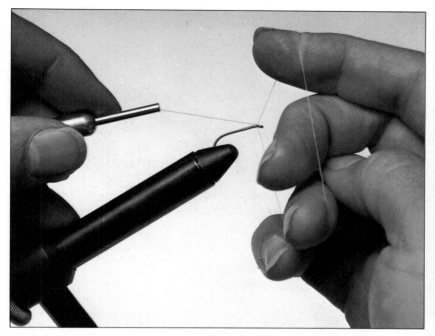

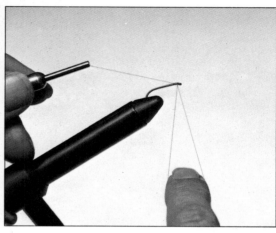

TOP LEFT The loop is now brought down below the hook with all three fingers, now moving to press on what is the front thread of the loop. The forefinger again takes the lead to bring the loop of thread up over the hook once more.

TOP RIGHT When four or five turns have been wrapped around the shank, the loop is brought down below the hook and just the forefinger and thumb can pinch the remains of the loop until it is pulled tight.

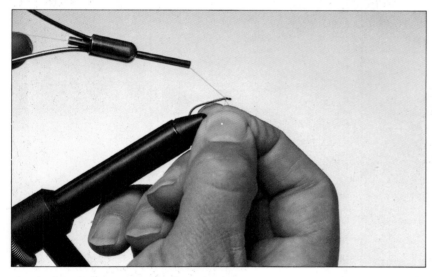

CENTRE LEFT Pull the bobbin gently and the loop will be pulled towards the hook shank until the forefinger and thumb can pinch the remains of the loop until it is pulled through.

BOTTOM LEFT Alternatively, you can use the dubbing needle to control the loop being pulled in tight.

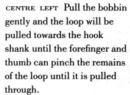

BOTTOM RIGHT Scissors cut off the thread and the completed whip finish is the most secure way to finish off a fly.

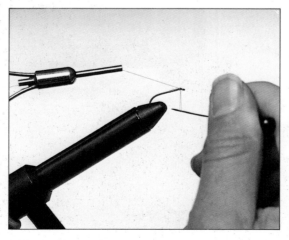

Making Your First Fly

Get to the stage of a hook held securely in the vice and the tying thread secured to the hook shank. We will start off with a pattern made from feather fibre for the body. It is better to start by doing this as you immediately get used to handling feather rather than strong wool. Take two fibres of peacock herl and cut off the curly end where the fibre was attached to the main quill and then line up the two cut ends in your left hand so that about half an inch of material projects from between your finger and thumb. Offer this up at an angle to the hook and just touching it.

Holding the bobbin in your right hand raise it up and round the hook and all the time maintain tension on the thread. As the thread comes up round the hook shank it will cross the ends of the two sections of peacock herl and trap them against the hook. Carry on round the hook shank with the thread and twice more wrap it round the peacock fibres. You will always be turning the thread over the hook away from your body in a clockwise motion.

Having secured the body material to the hook the usual step would be to take the tying thread up towards the eye of the hook and then wrap the body material round the shank. Peacock fibre is, however, rather a fragile material and the first fish caught on the fly will invariably cut one of the fibres with its teeth. Consequently, the fibre will then unravel and very shortly you have no fly.

We are now going to strengthen the body material of this fly by taking the two fibres of herl into the right hand along with the tying thread and commence winding them all round the hook shank, working first down towards the bend and then back up towards the eye so as to build up a nice, chunky body. After about the fourth turn round the hook you will notice that the herls are twisting and that the thread is twisted with them. As you wrap this twist round the hook, each herl is being trapped by the other and by the thread, so if the herl should become cut it cannot unravel because it is trapped by so many turns. This is the way to get a good, strong fly which will last for more than one fish.

At this juncture I am going to stress the first of the points about proportioning.

It is vital that as you attach each piece of material to the hook you take note of how it will appear at the final stage. For example, even with such a seemingly simple operation as attaching two strands of peacock herl and making a body, it is important that the body starts and finishes at defined points on the shank of the hook. There is only going to be a herl body on this fly, so the twist should be taken down to the bend of the hook to fill the level section of shank. It should finish at the end with sufficient room left to make a hackle and a whip finish.

Probably, the most common mistake you will make is to leave insufficient room at the head of the fly; this not only makes it very difficult to finish the fly but it appears very crude and introduces a weak point where it can become undone.

A correctly constructed and proportioned fly not only catches fish more efficiently bit it 'looks' right. You will soon be like every other fly tyer: when a fellow angler looks in your box and asks where you buy your flies you will look smug and say 'Actually, I make my own!'. So now we have a well-tied body of peacock herl on the hook and if we add a hackle the fly will be born and usable.

For this, our first-ever fly, it is going to be a wet fly that will be fished

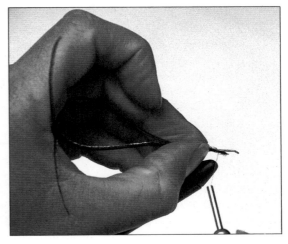

TOP Prepare the peacock herl for tying in.

ABOVE Tie the herls to the hook shank.

OPPOSITE Surrounded by the materials of his craft, this fly dresser puts the final touches on a beautiful, fully dressed Durham Ranger salmon fly.

underwater and therefore the hackle to use is one from a hen neck. It will easily absorb water and sink, whereas a cock hackle would be all stiff and spiky and prevent the fly from penetrating the surface film.

Use a dyed black hen hackle and the fly will be a recognized pattern called a Black and Peacock Spider, a very effective artificial. Look at your black hen neck and you will see that at the base, which is the top of the bird's head, the hackles are short and have short fibres, while those at the other end of the neck are much longer and have correspondingly longer fibres.

A hackle must be selected that will have the correct fibre length for the size of fly being tied. Proportioning again!

Refer to the drawings of a standard wet fly and you will see that the hackle fibre length is slightly longer than the total shank length. Therefore we need a hackle with fibres of these proportions for the hook in the vice. Instead of randomly taking a hackle off the neck and finding that it is not right it is better to offer the whole neck up to the hook and bend out individual hackles until you have one that is right and then pluck it off the neck. Do this by gripping the hackle at its base and pulling it towards the base of the neck, away from its natural growth line, and it will pop out of the skin.

The hackle must now be prepared before it can be tied to the hook and this involves stripping off the downy fluff from either side of the base of the stem so that only the actual fibres proper are left. Do this by gripping the fluff each side of the stem and pulling down and away from the stem.

Now hold the prepared hackle up between finger and thumb and you will see that it has a distinct curvature and a face side which is on the outside of the curve. If the hackle is tied to the hook and wound so that the curve points towards the eye, the fibres will all slope that way and the fly will look unnatural and oppose the water as it is retrieved, rather than envelop it by curving over the hook.

Correctly positioning the hackle before attaching it to the hook overcomes this problem and it is a matter of offering the prerpared hackle up to the hook so that its face is towards you and the natural curve of the feather is over the top of the hook. Lok at the photograph above and it is very clear.

Now trap the hackle stem against the hook shank in the same way as you did the peacock herl stems. The tying thread should be on the hook-eye side of the hackle at this point.

This is where we introduce another tool, the hackle pliers. They act like a spare pair of hands and grip the end of the hackle very firmly. Hold them in line with the stem of the hackle and grip the last quarter-inch.

Now wind the hackle round the hook shank in the same direction as the tying thread, i.e. over the body going away from you and in a clockwise direction. Do not twist the hackle but keep its face side pointing at the hook and eye and make each turn at the same place on the shank. Do not let it wander about to cover a long area, keep it compact.

Do about four turns of the hackle and now finish with the hackle pointing down from the shank. Cross it over in front of the tying thread and lift the thread up and over the hook to trap the end of the hackle against the hook. Do a couple of turns over the hackle and you can now carefully cut it off. Use your best scissors and snip the stem close to the hook, but be careful you do not cut the thread as well.

The fly is now virtually complete but before you do the whip fiish, which you learnt in a previous section, you will need to tidy up the head

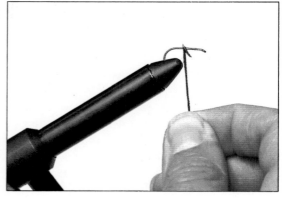

TOP Herls and tying thread held together.

ABOVE Winding on the body and the twist develops.

BELOW A correctly proportioned body with room left for the pattern being tied.

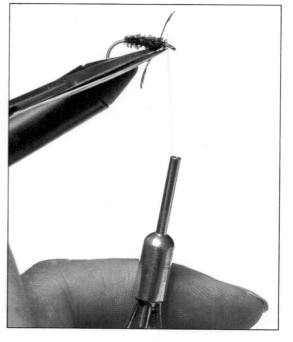

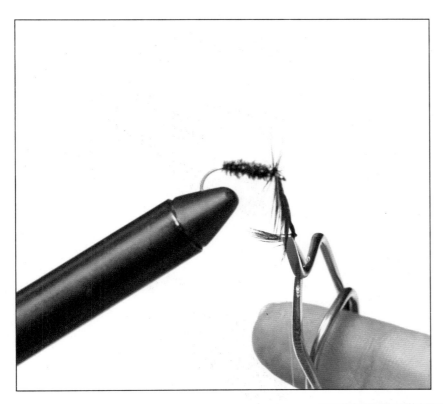

LEFT Winding the hackle with the aid of hackle pliers.

RIGHT The natural curve of the feather shows the correct way to tie it in.

LEFT The wrong way to tie in a hackle.

RIGHT Cutting off the waste tip of the hackle.

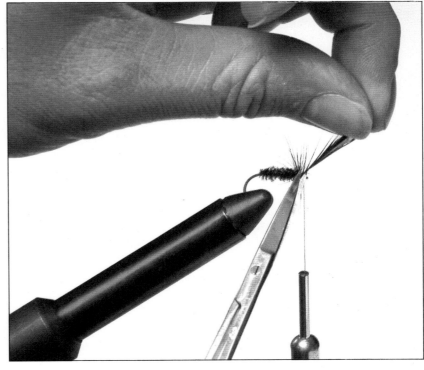

of the fly because there are almost always a few odd bits of hackle fibre sticking out at the wrong angle, making the whip finish difficult to carry out.

I tidy up by touching the tips of my thumb and first two fingers of my left hand together, leaving a small gap between them. Then slip this finger/thumb pinch over the eye of the fly and slide it backwards down the body of the fly. Bits of the fibre will be stroked backwards, allowing you to take a couple of turns of the thread over this last section to trap them in a backward-sloping profile and leave the way clear for the whip finish.

That is it, your first fly! Now go out and catch a fish on it.

A final professional effect can be created by applying a coating of dope to the whipping. There are several proprietary products for this final stage, some take the form of a varnish which sets like rock and is called head cement. The kind of dope used by model-aircraft makers is perfectly all right for the job and if you apply it with the point of the dubbing needle it will go on very evenly and accurately. Try putting on a layer of black dope and when it is dry add a layer of clear. This gives a shiny head to the fly just like those commercial patterns.

You have now learned to make a simple fly and can put on a herl body and a wet fly hackle, so now it is time to move on to another stage.

TOP Attaching the hackle to the hook shank.

ABOVE Varnishing the whip.

Additional Materials in Common Usage

Hackles from either cock or hen come in a wide variety of natural colours as well as the myriad of dyed ones available and a good fly tying collection should include:

Grizzle, white, badger, honey and cree cock necks

White, ginger and greenwell hen

Dyed cock and hen in shades of olive, red, claret, orange, blue, green and yellow

Natural and dyed black, yellow and bleached white deer hair

Marabou plumes (in fact from the domestic turkey) in a wide range of dyed colours

Ostrich herl in a range of colours

Partridge feathers, English and French

A hare's mask, ie the complete face of the hare for a range of excellent dubbing material

Other tinsels such as oval silver and gold and copper wire

Golden pheasant crest and neck feathers

Dyed hairs in various colours, squirrel, bucktail and goat

Condor substitute, large quill feathers dyed in various colours

Manmade materials such as chenille, raffene, latex, swannudaze, flashabou, polythene and a wide range of other items used by fly tyers

Wing quills from starling, grouse, woodcock and speckled hen

Flank feathers from teal and wood duck

Bronze mallard feathers and, from the same bird, the blue wing coverts

A whole range of dubbing materials, some natural some manmade and in a wide variety of colours.

This list may seem an intimidating one but once you are dedicated to fly tying you will inevitably accumulate most of the items on this list and a good many more!

ABOVE A wide selection
of feathers which
will enable many patterns to
be tied

LEFT A dubbing twister.

BELOW The Gallows
tool for parachute hackles.

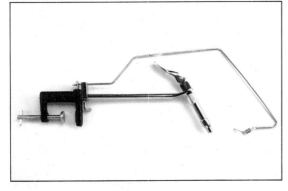

Fly tying is all about inventiveness and you will try all manner of materials in an attempt to find that deadly, sure-fire, never-failing pattern.

ADDITIONAL TOOLS

At the beginning of this chapter I suggested that you acquire two pairs of scissors, one for feather and one for tinsel and so on. Now that you are well into fly tying I suggest that you buy a really first-class pair and just keep them for your better work with small flies.

A dubbing twister is a very useful gadget for tying dubbed bodies with short-fibres furs such as mole or hare's ear. It will more than earn its keep.

A hair stacker is a tube into which you slip long hairs which are to form wings and so on, and then by tapping the tube you can ensure that all the ends of the hairs are lined up.

A gallows tool enables parachute hackles to be tied with relative ease and it is a worth-while addition to your equipment.

Being an inventive lot, fly tyers are forever bringing out 'new' gadgets but you will rarely find professional tyers using any others than those tools I have listed. If a pro does not use a tool, be sure that it is not worth buying.

Standard Wet Flies

This last section comprises a broad selection of flies from the four categories of patterns. The text lists suggested hook sizes and the component tying of the pattern, along with a brief description of best conditions for using each fly.

Changing from hen to cock hackles will convert the patterns to simple dry flies. An all black fly with a silver rib becomes a Williams Favourite. Change the tail to red wool and palmer up a cock hackle and you have a Zulu, a red wool body and tail with a palmered, red game, cock hackle becomes a Soldier Palmer. You will soon concoct your own variations on the basic theme and believe me – they will catch fish.

OPPOSITE Although necessity for conservation rightly prohibits the use of rare materials once thought essential to successful fly tying, the range of 'authorised' materials is still large enough for the creative fly dresser.

~~~~~ LIGHT CAHILL ~~~~~

A long established American wet fly, equally effective in dry or nymph form; all tyings are included here because of its all round fish-taking ability.

Hook: 16-8 standard shank
Tail: cream hackle fibres
Body: cream seals fur sub
Hackle: ginger hen hackle tied false
Wing: wood duck fibres

~~~~~~ ALEXANDRA ~~~~~~~

This is a showy fly which imitates nothing and yet in true wet fly mould it is a remarkable fish catcher. Many times the colour combination of red, black and silver will occur in fly patterns.

Hook: 6-12 standard shank
Tail: red feather fibres
Body: flat silver tinsel
Hackle: black hen tied false
Wing: peacock sword feathers with slips of red feather alongside

~~ PARMACHENE BELLE ~~

An attractor wet fly that is pleasing to look at, demanding to tie and deadly when fished in bright sun and clear water. Use a long leader and fish it very slowly just under the surface.

Hook: 12-8 standard shank
Tail: red and white cock hackle fibres
Body: yellow floss with flat gold rib
Hackle: red and white cock fibres tied false
Wing: married strips of red and white goose

~~~ WICKHAM'S FANCY ~~~

A pattern that fishes well when caddis flies are on the move or as a general attractor all year round and the basis of the early stages in this book.

Hooks: 16-8 standard shank
Tail: red game cock hackle fibres
Body: gold tinsel with wire rib
Hackle: palmered red game cock
Wing: grey mallard

~~~~~~~ INVICTA ~~~~~~~

Another famous pattern for when the adult caddis/sedge are on the move, particularly in the evenings. Not an easy pattern to tie well; an excellent test of skills.

Hooks: 14-8 standard shank
Tail: golden pheasant crest
Body: dubbed yellow/amber seals fur sub with a palmered red game cock hackle and an oval gold rib
Hackle: blue jay tied false
Wing: hen pheasant centre tail

~ TEAL BLUE AND SILVER ~

Not many patterns use blue but it is very attractive to fresh migratory fish and this fly is a special for sea trout, the migratory form of browns.

Hooks: 14-8 standard shank
Tail: golden pheasant tippets
Body: silver tinsel with wire rib
Hackle: blue hen tied false
Wing: teal flank feathers

~~~~~ PETER ROSS ~~~~~

Just look at the colour combination again but this time combined with the striped effect, which is another trigger to a predatory fish mind.

Hooks: 16-8 standard shank
Tail: golden pheasant tippets
Body: 2/3 silver tinsel, 1/3 red wool or seals fur sub, all ribbed with silver wire
Hackle: black hen tied false
Wing: teal flank feather

~MALLARD AND CLARET~

Particularly good early in the season on river or lake and when chironomids are hatching.

Hooks: 16-8 standard shank
Tail: golden pheasant tippets
Body: claret seals fur sub or wool with gold rib
Hackle: claret or black hen
Wing: bronze mallard

~~~~~~~~~~ ZULU ~~~~~~~~~~

The black, red, and silver combination again. A great favourite in waters that are poor food producers and where the fish have to be opportunist feeders.

Hooks: 16-8 standard shank
Tail: red wool
Body: black wool or seals fur sub
Hackle: black cock, sometimes palmered

~~~~~~~~~ BIBIO ~~~~~~~~~~

Just how many permutations are possible. Here is another deadly pattern using the primary trout colours.

Hooks: 12-8 standard shank
Body: black seals fur sub or wool with small red section in the middle
Hackle: black cock palmered with a silver wire rib

~~~~ SOLDIER PALMER ~~~~

A marvellous fly for the top dropper position on a wet fly cast as if fished in the surface film it resembles an insect struggling to emerge.

Hooks: 16-8 standard shank
Body: dubbed red seals fur substitute
Hackle: red game cock palmered with gold wire rib

~~~ WATSON'S FANCY ~~~

Yet another in the black/red/silver mould and a real test of a fly tier's skills. I once had to make 12 dozen of this one in size 16 for an order; what a job that was.

Hook: 14-8 standard shank
Tail: golden pheasant crest
Body: half black, half red wool with silver rib
Hackle: black hen tied false
Wing: slips of black crow with cheeks of jungle cock

~ WOODCOCK AND GREEN ~

A tried and tested pattern that is very good when fished in the upper layers during a hatch from stillwater.

Hook: 16-8 standard shank
Tail: golden pheasant tippets
Body: green seals fur sub ribbed with gold tinsel
Hackle: pale green tied false
Wing: woodcock wing quills

~~~~ SILVER INVICTA ~~~~

A look at the best flies on fishery reports will see this pattern come to prominence in July when the coarse fish are around and it is an excellent imitation of a pin fry as well as being a good all round pattern.

Hook: 14-8 standard shank
Tail: golden pheasant crest
Body: silver tinsel with palmered red game cock hackle and wire rib
Hackle: blue jay fibres tied false
Wings: hen pheasant centre tail feathers

~~~~ BLACK PENNELL ~~~~

One of the best flies I know when chironomids are hatching on lakes; in larger sizes it takes sea trout and tied bushy is a great dapping fly.

Hook: 14-8 standard shank
Tail: golden pheasant tippets
Body: butt of silver wire then ribbed over black floss
Hackle: black cock tied long in the fibre

~ CINNAMON AND GOLD ~

This lovely old pattern is not only a good fish catcher it's also good to look at and satisfying to tie.

Hook: 12-8 standard shank
Tail: golden pheasant tippets
Body: flat gold tinsel
Hackle: ginger cock hackle fibres tied false
Wing: cinnamon hen wing quills

~~~ GREENWELLS GLORY ~~~

This fly has been around a long time and caught many trout for anglers all over the world and I am quite sure will continue to do so as long as there are trout to be caught.

Hook: 14-8 standard shank
Tail: greenwell hen hackle fibres (ginger with black centre and sometimes omitted)
Body: yellow tying thread darkened with wax and ribbed with golden wire
Hackle: hen greenwell tied false
Wing: starling dyed brownish green

~~~~~~~ DUNKELD ~~~~~~~~

Tied in larger sizes and even up to salmon size this is a great fly for a bit of flash and glitter, especially good on sunny days worked through the top layers of water.

Hooks: 16-8 standard shank
Tail: golden pheasant crest
Body: gold tinsel with wire rib
Hackle: hot orange cock tied false
Wing: bronze mallard

~~~~~~~ BUTCHER ~~~~~~~~

Once again the combination of black, red and silver, this is not an easy pattern to tie well because of the difficult wing material, but it is an excellent fish catcher.

Hooks: 16-8 standard shank
Tail: red ibis substitute
Body: silver tinsel with wire rib
Hackle: black hen tied false
Wing: blue mallard

Lures

~~~~~ JERSEY HERD ~~~~~~

An English reservoir pattern attributed to Tom Ivens. An excellent all-round fly, but at its best around fry time at the back end of the year.

Hook: 6-20 longshank
Tail, back and head: peacock herl
Body: copper coloured tinsel
Hackle: hot orange cock wound full

~~~~~ LIGHT SPRUCE ~~~~~

A commonly used streamer pattern for trout on the West coast of America but almost unknown in the UK.

Hook: 6-10 longshank
Tail: peacock sword feather
Body: red floss and peacock herl
Hackle: badger cock wound full
Wing: badger cock hackles tied streamer style

~~~~ SILVER DARTER ~~~~

An American favourite that has found success all over the world and is especially good in broken water.

Hook: 6-10 longshank
Tail: silver mylar tubing
Hackle: peacock sword feather

~~~ MUDDLER MINNOW ~~~

Originally created by Don Gapen in the USA to imitate a small minnow in the streams, and now in a wide variety of options. Effective bumbled over the bottom or stripped over the surface.

Hook: 6-10 longshank
Tail: oak turkey (use hen pheasant centre tail as a sub)
Body: flat gold tinsel with wire rib
Wing: grey squirrel sheathed with oak turkey
Head: deer hair flared and clipped

OPPOSITE The plant life that flourishes in sheltered areas, such as under bridges, are home to many of the insects that attract fish. This angler on the River Yeo, in Somerset has chosen his position carefully.

~~ BLACK AND ORANGE ~~ MARABOU

One of Taff Price's inventions that has taken a great many fish by exploiting the amazing mobility of marabou.

Hook: 6-10 longshank
Tail: orange cock hackle fibres
Body: flat gold tinsel with oval rib
Hackle: orange cock hackle fibres
Wing: black marabou sometimes with jungle cock cheeks

~~~~~ MRS SIMPSON ~~~~~

An unusual style of fly of which there are a number of varieties all of which involved feathers tied in along the sides of the hook. Gives a very dense silhouette to the fly.

Hook: 6-10 longshank
Tail: black squirrel tail
Body: red floss
Hackle: three pairs of cock pheasant body feathers tied in at intervals along the shank

~~~~ YELLOW MATUKA ~~~~

A New Zealand pattern which catches well anywhere but especially where trout feed on bait fish in lakes.

Hook: 6-10 longshank
Tail and wing: well marked hen greenwell feathers
Body: yellow floss ribbed with oval gold
Hackle: hen greenwell

~~~~ WOOLLY BUGGER ~~~~

Very simple pattern and yet quite deadly, especially in cold water when fished low and deep. Must be the easiest to tie.

Hook: 10-6 longshank
Tail: black hackle fibres
Body: black chenille with palmered black hackle

~~~~ BLACK MARABOU ~~~~ MUDDLER

Yet another muddler variant and, surprise, surprise, here is the red, black and silver combination again.

Hook: 6-10 longshank
Tail: red feather fibres
Body: flat silver tinsel with wire rib
Wing: black marabou fibres
Head: deer hair flared and clipped

~~~~ ACE OF SPADES ~~~~

Essentially a black lure variant but tied matuka style with an overwing so as to give a solid profile and prevent the wing tangling under the hook bend.

Hook: 6-10 longshank
Tail and back: hen hackles dyed black
Rib: oval silver tinsel
Hackle: guinea fowl tied false
Over wing: bronze mallard

~~~~ DAVES SCULPIN ~~~~

A muddler variation which works well when fished slow and deep, particularly for older, well established fish that have turned completely predatory.

Hook: 10-4 longshank
Body: creamy yellow wool
Wing: matuka style cree cock
Rib: oval gold
Over wing: brown squirrel fibres
Fins: hen pheasant body feathers
Head: bands of coloured deer hair tied muddler style

~~~~ DOG NOBBLER ~~~~

This is a modern variation of an early type of jig fly and which is very effective on newly stocked trout. The undulating action of the tail induced by the lead head makes the fly swim enticingly.

Hook: 6-10 standard or longshank with a split shot crimped and glued to the head
Tail: bunch of marabou fibres, any colour and related to rest of fly
Body: chenille with palmered cock hackle and tinsel over rib
Head: eye effect painted on the shot

~~~~~ BLACK GHOST ~~~~~

Wherever fish feed on fry the black ghost will catch them. It is a truly excellent pattern from the US.

Hook: 6-10 longshank
Tail: yellow hackle fibres or golden pheasant crest
Body: black floss ribbed with silver oval or flat
False hackle: yellow cock hackle fibres
Wing: four white cock hackle fibres tied streamer-style

~~~~~~ WHISKY ~~~~~~~

Orange is a wonderful colour for rainbow trout, especially in the summer months. It can provoke the fish into quite literally attacking the fly. The whisky fly is a great lure and a simple pattern to tie.

Hook: 6-12 longshank
Tail: hot orange cock hackle fibres
Body: gold tinsel with rib of flou orange floss
Hackle: hot orange cock tied false
Wing: orange calf or squirrel tail

~~~~~ SWEENY TODD ~~~~~

A Richard Walker invention using the time-honoured colour combination of red, black and silver to make a modern and highly effective lure.

Hook: 6-20 longshank
Body: black floss with oval silver rib
Collar: neon magenta floss
Hackle: red cock fibres tied false
Wing: black squirrel tail

~~~~~ MICKY FINN ~~~~~

This is a great pattern for the aggressive rainbow when the water warms up and they will chase a fly; but it also works well for many other species, specially when the water is coloured.

Hook: 6-10 longshank
Body: Flat silver ribbed with oval silver
Wing: in three parts, yellow, red and yellow bucktail, squirrel for the smaller sizes

~~~~~ MUNRO KILLER ~~~~~

A hair wing version of modern salmon flies that is easy to make and every bit as effective as complicated feather wing patterns.

Hook: 4-12 up eye salmon iron

Tag: oval gold

Body: black floss with oval gold rib

Hackle: hot orange cock and dyed blue guinea fowl

Wing: yellow bucktail with black over, squirrel for smaller flies

~~~~~ BLUE CHARM ~~~~~

This is a recognised salmon fly but in reality is just a lure and shows how salmon flies can be simply tied with feather wings. Actually quite difficult to get well proportioned.

Hook: 4-12 up eye salmon

Tag: oval silver

Tail: golden pheasant crest and black ostrich as a butt

Body: black floss with oval silver rib

Hackle: blue cock

Wing: bronze mallard with teal over wing and golden pheasant crest as a topping

~~~~~ POLYSTICKLE ~~~~~

Another Richard Walker pattern which is intended to imitate a small fish and show its translucence. It comes under the general heading of lures and as you can see uses very little natural material in its tying.

Hook: 6-12 longshank

Tail and back: raffene

Body: black floss rib over silver then red floss and all over wound with strip of clear polythene

Hackle: red or orange cock hackle tied false

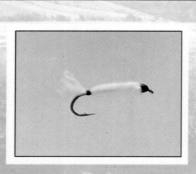

~~~~~~ BABY DOLL ~~~~~~

So called because it was apparently first tied using the white wool from baby's clothes, this pattern is tied in a fish shape, but it relies on the glow of the white wool to attract fish. White has always been a good lure colour, especially at fry time.

Hook: 6-10 long or standard shank
Tail, body, back: all of white 'baby' wool

~~~~~~ APPETIZER ~~~~~~

A white based English pattern which is an excellent lure for fry feeders and makes use of the mobility of marabou for its enticing action.

Hook: 6-10 longshank
Tail: mixed fibres of silver mallard, orange and green cock hackle fibres
Body: white chenille ribbed with silver oval
Hackle: same mix as tail and tied false
Wing: white marabou with grey squirrel over

~~~ ROYAL COACHMAN ~~~ BUCKTAIL

A North American variation on an old pattern which has turned an already good fly into an excellent lure.

Hook: 6-10 longshank
Tail: golden pheasant tippetts
Body: red floss with ends of peacock herl
Hackle: brown cock tied false
Wing: white bucktail fibres

OPPOSITE The angler equipped with waders is able to pursue the most reluctant of fish.

Nymphs

~~~~~~ PVC NYMPH ~~~~~~

A John Goddard pattern, the abdomen is covered with stretched PVC to give the nymph a lifelike appearance. Very good on rivers when a hatch is on.

Hook: 12-16 standard shank
Tail: olive dyed feather fibre
Abdomen: olive feather with stretched PVC over
Thorax: olive feather fibre with brownish feather fibre wing case

~~~~~ BLACK NYMPH ~~~~~

One of the most basic tyings you can do for a nymph and absolutely invaluable to have in the box. Black works anywhere in the world for the fly fisher.

Hook: 8-14 standard shank
Tail: black hackle fibres
Body: black seals fur sub ribbed with silver wire
Thorax: black seals fur sub with grey feather fibre over

~~~~ DAMSEL NYMPH ~~~~

It's stretching credulity to call this fly an imitation of the damsel nymph but it's a fact that trout feeding on the natural will take this pattern very well indeed.

Hook: 8-12 longshank
Tail: green hackle fibres
Body: seals fur substitute, multi-colour mix
Rib: gold oval
Hackle: golden olive dyed partridge

~~~~~~~ ZUG BUG ~~~~~~~~

A generalized nymph pattern that originated in America and has since proved its worth in all waters that hold trout. It can be very good when fished weighted.

Hook: 10-14 standard shank
Tail: peacock sword
Body: peacock herl, ribbed flat silver
Hackle: brown hen
Wing: wood duck

~~~~ SWANNUNDAZE ~~~~
STONEFLY

An excellent pattern that makes full use of the translucence obtained by the use of swannundaze, a plastic which is flat one side and oval on the other.

Hook: 6-8 longshank, bent to suggest the humped pupa

Tail: brown goose biots

Abdomen: mixed golden yellow and grey seals fur sub dubbed heavily and ribbed with amber swannundaze

Thorax: similar dubbing mix with the wing cases being formed by laying a brown speckled partridge feather along the back and overlaying a striped partridge feather

~~~~~~~ PRINCE ~~~~~~~

An interesting fly in that it looks 'buggy' and yet actually resembles nothing specific. The white feather slips seem to act as an attractant to the fish.

Hook: 8-12 standard shank

Tail: brown goose biot

Body: peacock herl with flat gold rib

Hackle: brown hen

Horns: slips of white goose or swan

~~~ MONTANA NYMPH ~~~

A dressing of the Stone Fly Larva initiated in Montana and now used worldwide. A general-purpose pattern where the Stone Fly does not occur and in Europe it is little other than a variant of the black lure.

Hook: 12-8 longshank, often weighted

Tail: black cock hackle tips or bunch of black cock hackle fibres

Abdomen: black chenille

Thorax: yellow chenille with variants using fluo green, white or orange

Wing case: black chenille

Hackle: Black cock wound through the thorax

~~~~ GOLD RIBBED ~~~~
HARE'S EAR

This is a fly that catches any trout that is feeding on ephemerid (mayfly) nymphs, and also works as a general nymph pattern right throughout the year.

Hook: 8-16 standard shank

Tail: ginger hackle fibres or longer hairs from a hare's mask

Body: dubbed hare's ear ribbed with gold tinsel

Thorax: dubbed hare's ear picked out with feather fibre wing case

~~~~~ CASED CADDIS ~~~~~

Larvae of the stonefly (caddis) make up the greater part of a trout's diet, especially in the early season, and imitations of the larval form fished along the bottom are very successful.

Hook: 8-12 longshank
Body: blue underfur from a rabbit dubbed onto silver tinsel chenille and wound
Head: black ostrich herl

~~~~~ TEENY NYMPH ~~~~~

Invented by Oregon's steelhead king, Jim Teeny, this fly was to be a broad band pattern suitable for all species and simple to tie so there would be no fear of fishing it in snaggy places. Tied in a variety of colours and only using rooster (cock pheasant) tail fibres.

Hook: 12 short shank to 2 longshank
Body, false hackles: tail feather fibres from a rooster (cock pheasant) sometimes tied with a wing of the same material on the larger hooks

~~~~~ GREEN BITCH ~~~~~ CREEK NYMPH

A modern American tying using living rubber for its action; a general stone fly pattern.

Hook: 6-10 longshank
Tail: two pieces of living rubber
Body: woven from fluo green and black chenille
Thorax: black chenille with red game cock hackle palmered through it
Head: two more pieces of living rubber

~ COCKWILLS RED BROWN ~

Based on a reservoir pattern by the late Tom Ivens and intended to represent the coloration of the male stickleback at breeding time, this fly has proved to be a very good general-purpose nymph for most stillwaters.

Hook: 10 longshank
Tail, back and head: four fibres of peacock herl
Body: copper golfingering ribbed with a strand of brown ostrich herl and copper wire
Thorax: two turns of neon magenta chenille

~~ GREEN THORAX PTN ~~

A variant on the pheasant tail series and using green fluo which attracts trout so well. Used as a general purpose nymph or fished fast at fry time.

Hook: 8-12 longshank
Tail: pheasant tail fibres
Body: pheasant tail fibres ribbed with copper wire
Thorax: fluo green floss with pheasant fibres over
Hackle: ginger cock tied false

~~ COLONEL'S CREEPER ~~

An all-purpose nymph that would make an excellent stonefly imitation and has found great success in English stillwaters.

Hook: 8-10 longshank
Tail: bunch of olive dyed rabbit fur
Body: weighted along the sides of the hook to widen it then dubbed olive seals fur sub ribbed with nylon
Thorax: dressed upside down and made with two wing cases of varnished raffene and legs of olive goose biots in among the dubbed olive seals fur sub

~~~~~~ LEAD BUG ~~~~~~

One of the author's patterns and designed for use on large fish which can be targetted in clear water. It gives a very approximate suggestion of a nymph, with its segmented body and thorax hump, and is intended to sink very rapidly, yet not be too heavy.

Hook: 10 to 12 standard shank
Tail: olive floss
Abdomen: fine lead wire
Thorax, wing case and leg stubs: olive floss

~~~~ GOLDEN SHRIMP ~~~~

The shrimp is a drab greenish or brown hue, although when changing its skin it is very much paler; many anglers feel that the golden shrimp somehow appears to be vulnerable to the trout. Whatever the truth, the fly is very successful.

Hook: 10 or 12 standard shank, a Sedge pattern is very good
Tail: fibres of golden olive cock hackle
Body: golden olive seals fur or substitute
Hackle: palmered golden olive cock
Back: yellow dyed latex
Rib: gold wire

~~~~~ LIGHT CAHILL ~~~~~

A truly excellent general-purpose nymph for all epheremid/mayfly patterns in streams. North American in origin and no fly box should be without it.

Hook: 10-18 standard shank
Tail: wood duck fibres
Body: creamy seals fur substitute
Hackle: ginger hen fibres
Wing case: wood duck

~~~~ GREEN CHOMPER ~~~~

A remarkably easy pattern to tie and it can suggest all manner of aquatic life. The fish certainly think it looks edible and the colour can be varied according to water and season.

Hook: 10-14 standard shank
Back: raffene
Body: ostrich herl

OPPOSITE This 29 lb (13 kg) salmon was caught in the River Exe, Somerset.

Dry Flies

~~~~~ ROYAL WULFF ~~~~~

One of Lee Wulff's all time greats and a wonderful general purpose dry that rides rough water very well and is taken by all species.

Hook: 8-12 standard shank
Tail: black squirrel hair
Body: red floss with peacock herl either end
Wings: white calf tail
Hackle: two red game cock hackles

~~~ CINNAMON SEDGE ~~~

A very effective broad band sedge pattern, not just for when the actual cinnamon sedge is hatching. Equally effective on rivers or lakes.

Hook: 10-14 up eye
Body: cinnamon feather fibre with palmered ginger cock hackle and gold wire rib
Wings: cinnamon hen quills
Hackle: ginger cock hackle

~~ FRENCH PARTRIDGE ~~ MAYFLY

An all-time English favourite for the annual mayfly carnival when the trout gorge themselves on this large insect. There may be more efficient patterns, but this one is so pretty.

Hook: special mayfly 8-10 longshank
Tail: cock pheasant fibres
Body: natural raffia ribbed with red thread and an olive cock hackle and gold wire
Hackle: French partridge flank feather

~~~ DADDY LONG LEGS ~~~ (CRANE FLY)

A large terrestrial that trout love to eat and which in late summer can hatch in enormous numbers.

Hook: 8-12 longshank
Body: detached end of closely bunched dyed deer hair
Legs: knotted cock pheasant tail fibres
Wings: cree hackle points
Hackle: two ginger cock hackles wound full

~~~ ELK HAIR HOPPER ~~~

Hoppers are a great fly to fish in the summer in the USA when they are cast at the edges of the stream. Now they are being used in Europe but more as general purpose dries on lakes.

Hook: 8-12 longshank
Tail: red dyed squirrel hair
Body: yellow floss ribbed with clipped Grizzle hackle
Wing: bunch of elk hair
Hackle: two cree cock hackles

~~~~~ LIGHT CAHILL ~~~~~

Thought to be at least a hundred years old, this pattern is very effective when the paler ephemerids are hatching, especially in the evening when it is easy to see.

Hook: 12-16 standard shank
Tail: cream hackle fibres
Body: cream seals fur substitute
Wings: wood duck
Hackle: cream cock hackle

~~~~ YELLOW HUMPY ~~~~

A wonderful floater for rough water, originally from the freestone rivers of Western America.

Hook: 10-14 standard shank
Tail: moose fibres
Body: yellow floss with the moose fibres tied over the top
Wing: ends of a bunch of moose fibres
Hackle: two grizzle cock hackles

~ STRADDLEBUG MAYFLY ~

Interesting variation for mayfly in that this pattern has an orange hackle which makes it stand out from all the others. It often gets taken when the fish are full to the gills with the natural.

Hook: 8-12 longshank
Tail: cock pheasant fibres
Body: natural raffia ribbed with gold wire
Hackle: two wound together, hot orange cock and summer duck feather
Head: peacock herl

OPPOSITE The lure of angling:
trout fishing in the idyllic
Devon countryside.

~RICHARD WALKER SEDGE~

*The ever inventive Richard Walker produced
this pattern to have a sedge (caddis) profile; the
long hackle was so that the fly could be stripped
back over the surface to imitate the adults
skittering motion.*

Hook: 8-12 standard shank
Butt: hot orange floss
Body: cock pheasant fibres
Wing: red game cock hackle fibres
Hackle: red game cock hackle, long fibred

~~~~ BLACK BIVISIBLE ~~~~

*A fly that relies on merely suggesting an adult insect
by its straggly hackle and fuzzy outline. It has the
advantage of riding very well and being easy for the
angler to see and tie.*

Hook: 10-14 standard shank
Tail: black cock hackle fibres
Body: palmered black cock hackle
Hackle: white cock hackle

~~ DARK HENDRICKSON ~~

*A famous standard American dry that catches well
when the mayfly species hatch and scores on most
waters as a general pattern.*

Hook: 12-18 standard shank
Tail: dark dun or grey cock hackle fibres
Body: dubbed muskrat under fur
Wing: wood duck
Hackle: dark dun or grey cock hackle

~~~~~~ BLACK GNAT ~~~~~~

*A black dry fly is essential at times, especially in early
season when the natural hatches.*

Hook: 10-18 up eye
Tail: black cock hackle fibres
Body: black floss
Wings: grey mallard or starling
Hackle: black cock wound full

~~~~ QUILL GORDON ~~~~

A pattern from the Catskills in New York State, often used in the UK as an alternative to standard olive patterns when the natural is hatching.

Hook: 12-18 standard shank
Tail: light brown or grey cock hackle fibres
Body: stripped peacock quill
Wings: wood duck
Hackle: medium dun cock or grey cock

~~ BLUE WINGED OLIVE ~~

This imitation of a commonly occurring fly is a standard for when the fly hatches and is essential for anyone who fishes limestone (chalk) waters.

Hook: 14-16 standard shank
Tail: dark dun hackle fibres, grey will suffice
Body: dubbed olive grey fur
Wings: blue dun hackle tips
Hackle: dark dun cock or grey hackle

~~~~~~~ ADAMS ~~~~~~~

This American fly is now much used on English chalk streams, especially when olives are hatching. It also makes a good lake dry fly.

Hook: 10-20 standard shank
Tail: mixed brown and grizzle cock hackle fibres
Body: muskrat under fur dubbed
Wing: grizzle hackle tips
Hackle: mixed red game and grizzle

~~~ WICKHAMS FANCY ~~~

A flashy dry fly that serves well when there is a sedge hatch or when the water is rough and the sun bright when its wink of gold brings the fish up.

Hook: 16-8 standard shank
Tail: red game cock hackle fibres
Body: gold tinsel with palmered red game cock hackle and gold wire rib
Wings: grey mallard or starling
Hackle: red game cock hackle

~BLUE PHEASANT TAIL~

A fly of the rough water rivers which are fished best early in the year and will produce fish even when there is no hatch taking place.

Hook: 14-10 standard shank
Tail: pheasant tail fibres
Body: pheasant tail fibres with gold wire rib
Hackle: blue dun cock

~~~~~GREY DUSTER~~~~~

This is a wonderful pattern when all sorts of tiny smuts are on the water and trout are being 'difficult'. It will often fool the most crafty fish and yet is simplicity itself.

Hook: 18-12 standard shank
Body: dubbed rabbit under fur 'blueish grey'
Hackle: badger cock hackle 'white with black centre and tips'

~~LUNNS PARTICULAR~~

A classic Test fly and best when olive spinners are on the water but it serves for any fall of spent fly.

Hook: 16-14 up eye
Tail: fibres of red game cock hackle
Body: stripped red game cock hackle stem
Wings: blue dun hackle points tied spent
Hackle: red game cock hackle

OLIVE ELK ~~~~~WING CADDIS~~~~~

Quite an easy pattern to tie and the elk hair splay serves well to suggest the sedge (caddis) profile as well as making the fly float well.

Hook: 14-10 standard shank
Body: dubbed yellowish for substitute
Hackle: palmered red game cock hackle
Wing: elk hair with the butts lifted to make a head

SEA FISHING

Sea Fishing in British Waters

The British Isles while being politically part of Europe is not – yet – joined physically to the Continent, although billions of pounds sterling are being expended with this in mind. However, there are no deep seas between our islands and continental Europe because they both sit on one of the continental plates now known to move perhaps half an inch a year over the surface of the globe. The waters surrounding Britain constitute part of the shelf of our continental plate, and run down to about 200 fathoms, which is much shallower than the true deeps of 2,000 fathoms and more between the plates. It is in these shallow but rich waters where most of the sea angler's fishes are found. While there is no doubt of the sporting attraction of sea fishing the huge bonus is that almost everything caught is edible and welcome when the angler returns home. This statement should of course be qualified – conservation is as important in sea fishing as it is in freshwater.

The diversity of Britain's coastline means that there is an enormous variety in the kinds of sea fishing to be found in the seas round these comparatively small islands. The waters range from at times near-sub-tropical off Cornwall to the cold, grey seas of Northern Scotland; the Hebrides and the Shetlands, where that deep-water giant flattie the halibut can be found. Vast numbers of anglers go out in charter-boats day after day to seek the fish of the season, for unlike freshwater fishing which has its statutory closed seasons, in the seas the fish species them-selves create their own 'closed' periods when they are not to be caught for the simple reason that they are elsewhere.

The quality of shore fishing round Britain is legendary, and the sands and shingle beaches offer a variety of close-in marks from huge shellfish beds, cockle- and ragworm-inhabited mudflats, shelving beaches of sand, steeply angled shingle, rocks with intriguing gullies between them, to piers, groynes, seawalls, harbour walls, and brackish estuaries. All of these have their population of fishes for anglers to try for.

The piers that jut out from many holiday resorts are one of Britain's Victorian heritages. Their spidery ironwork, creaky planked walkways, 'fun palaces' and the odds and ends of entertainment are crowded with holidaymakers in summer and there is always a sprinkling of anglers perched on the extremities. But in winter the anglers have these places to themselves and since the piles and weed-covered supports hold life which fish feed upon, and the fish have become conditioned to expect edible bits and pieces dropped from the pier by man, some very accept-able fish can be caught here.

Strangely, one finds anglers at the very extreme end of the pier, fishing with long beachcasting rods in order to cast as far as possible. Most of the time any fish in the vicinity of the pier will be underneath it, seeking food items, not hovering some way off. The only real problem with pier fishing is that hooks and terminal tackle can easily be tapped in the struts and jumbled material below the surface. One method of avoid-ing this is to use a sea-type float to keep the baited hook clear of snags.

Like freshwater fishing, sea fishing is a form of escaping from the rat race – only more so. The coarse angler sitting by a quiet river, hearing nothing but the music of running water and bird-song, enjoys this as much as he does that first bite, and the initial sudden plunge of the float.

But the sea fisherman often has only the salt-smelling wind, the open sea and a 360-degree sky-lined horizon. He is also very much aware that the first, or any, bite may come from a fish that is as strong as a horse, a fish which may be 60 fathoms down and the size of a grand piano.

What of the sea? The first thing any skipper learns is that he must have total respect for it; not fear, but a wariness that tells him to take waterproofs and weather clothing even if the day dawns cloudless and the forecast is Fine. Heading out at 20 knots or so in fine weather soon has the craft well away from the shore. It is elementary, but must be said, that an hour's steaming out will take the same amount of time coming back, assuming there is no wind and the tide is an easy one. But add a Force 4 wind and an adverse spring tide and the time back can be doubled.

These matters must be considered by any skipper, whether professional or amateur. No one should take a boat out, whatever its size, without the knowhow and experience to handle the craft and himself properly. It is also unnecessary to say that unless the skipper has the elements of navigation, or at least knows where he is in relation to the nearest land (when it may well be out of sight), he should not be in control of a boat. Wasting the time of the rescue services is something the sea angler must never do.

Most of the above matters – except one – can be ignored by the beach or shore angler. The exception is preparation, nay, the anticipation of bad weather. No one can fish properly or efficiently if he or she is cold and wet, so adequate waterproof clothing must form part of the gear taken to the beach, together with sufficient food and drink to take him or her through the session. There are dangers in shore fishing; rocks will be slippery, and piers sometimes have open gratings on which the angler can stand which might be swamped by an unusually large wave.

BELOW Anglers on West Coast long range boats bring lots of gear with them. This is only a portion of one fisherman's tackle on the Royal Polaris from San Diego, California.

Sea Tackle

For years now, sea anglers have realized that for much of the time they have been fishing with gear that is too strong for the average sea species they are most likely to catch. 'There go the block-and-tackle boys!' was the jeer from coarse anglers on seeing a party of sea anglers setting out in a charter boat. Sometimes these comments were justified and everyone has reeled in some sea fish on line and hook that would cope with something much heavier without much trouble. But coarse anglers, too, have done this. How many specimen hunters after carp have cursed as yet another nuisance bream or roach has taken the bait and been reeled in on a stepped-up carp rod, 5lb b.s. line and Size 10 hook?

No angler could take a light freshwater rod, mount roach terminal tackle baited with lug, drop it down 10 fathoms, then hook, say, even a sizable pouting and get it to the surface. To begin with, his roach-suitable weight would never get anywhere near the seabed! With no tide it might eventually get there, but the first take from that middle pouting would be a disaster either for the hook, the line or the reel. With a few exceptions, close-in rock fishing perhaps, sea fishing demands sea fishing gear: rods that can stand the strain of hauling fish from the depths in a tide, line and hook that will cope with the fish, and a reel suitable for that line.

Sea-fishing rods were once stout weapons, some of which could cope with a sizable dinghy, and reels were large wooden centre-pins to match. But like all fishing, the tackle has been fined down with the arrival of

RIGHT An angler uses a Sabre 5½ft stand-up rod to fight a school tuna with the aid of a rod belt.

BELOW The Penn International 130 lever drag reel.

carbon and its derivatives for rods and reels. Strength is still there, though, and more dependable than rods of the past.

Boat rods range from about 5½ to 7ft (1.7 to 2m), with most being 6 to 6½ft (1.8 to 2m). Traditionally, they have had detachable wooden butts – but many now are one-piece with the blank running through the butt for strength. Actions vary from very light for bay fishing to more club-like where extra-heavy weights are required to hold bottom in deep water. In most cases it is the conditions, more than the size of the quarry, which determine the preferred rod action. Rods are rated by the size ranges of the lures and weights they'll handle, and the angler should pay close attention to that classification when making a selection.

Most boat rods are made of hollow fibreglass, though quite a few now incorporate some graphite. The latter material is most effective when used in the butt section to add stiffness. Solid glass rods are very common in this category as the material is inexpensive. Solid rods are heavy and have poor actions, but are also most unbreakable – making them ideal for charter-boat fishing. Since solids are built to sell in low price ranges, they tend to be equipped with the cheapest of components.

ROD RINGS

Whereas stainless steel rings have been virtually eliminated from freshwater rods, they remain very popular in saltwater. Tungsten carbide tips are often added to such rods, as the ring takes most of the abuse from monofilament lines. Tungsten carbide is also the standard for all rings when wire line is used, as steel rings will be quickly cut by the metal line. Aluminium oxide rings (the norm in freshwater) have been catching on, and some of the best rods feature silicon carbide rings.

REELS

Conventional reels used for boat fishing do not have to be quite as well balanced as others since most aren't intended for casting. Even when casting is necessary, it usually isn't important to get a great deal of distance. Overhand casting is prohibited (for safety reasons) on most party boats, so experienced anglers soon become expert at underhand casting that can put a line or weight quite a distance away from competing lines. However, a practiced thumb is required if you are to avoid constant backlashes with this technique.

In addition to lever drags, some of the higher priced models now feature graphite sideplates and one-piece frames for both strength and lightness. Level-wind models are available, and are favoured in some areas and by a percentage of fishermen trolling with wire line.

The selected boat reel should balance with the rod and have adequate capacity for the fishing. In most cases, fishermen choose boat reels that are quite a bit larger than they need for most of their normal fishing in order to use the same model on the occasional trolling or deep-sea trip. However, that means holding more weight than necessary throughout most of your fishing – which doesn't make sense.

Boat reel gear ratios are usually low in order to provide power for bottom fishing or to reel-in trolled fish. However, you will want faster retrieve models for casting (particularly if you plan to retrieve metal lures at high speeds).

The reels used in sea fishing must withstand the stress of perhaps 200 yards (183m) of high-breaking strain being rewound while a heavy fish is fighting all the way which puts a great compression strain on the spool. In addition they are subject to the corrosive effect of sea-water. The

ABOVE Party boat anglers use conventional reels to catch such game and food fish as this big pollock, jigged off a Nantucket wreck.

LEFT Wire line has its own weight to get the bait down fast and at an acute angle. But it needs special rings, has no stretch and must be used carefully. Here it is used with a multiplier. The lures are Eddystone eels.

BELOW Multipliers for light sea fishing. The reel on the right is an Abu 7000, the large handle allowing a very fast rate of retrieve.

ABOVE A multiplier
with level-wind mechanism.
On retrieve the line is fed
smoothly along the spool by a
guide linked to the reel's
gear mechanism.

compression strains can be alleviated to a great extent by pumping the fish, but the sea-water will stay until it is washed off. The nylon line, always wound under some tension, should be pulled onto another spare reel, washed and left to dry.

The multiplier is now in universal use for boat fishing. It has replaced the old wooden centre-pins with their huge-diameter spools. These looked very impressive, and in the hands of an expert were very effective in retrieving line at speed. But the multiplier of today is stronger, lighter and more resistant to salt corrosion. It also has star drags, brakes, line-guides and often lugs so that the reel and the rod can be attached to the angler when he is playing a particularly strong fish, which eases the strain on the arms. Fixed-spool reels are in use too, in a much smaller capacity. Their easy casting facility is helpful when spinning for bass or mackerel.

As in all kinds of fishing, reels designed for various kinds of sea fishing have been developed. The shark-hunter does not want a reel holding 200 yards (183m) of 15lb (6.8kg) b.s. line. He wants one that can hold sufficient high-breaking strain line to cope with a big shark. One such reel is – or was, for it is no longer made – a reel made by Hardys which held 800 yards (732m) of 80lb (36kg) b.s. line. This is the kind of capacity for shark reels. For lesser species there are many fine reels holding plenty of 20, 50, 80lb (9, 22.6, 36kg) b.s. line, enough for most bottom-fishing species.

ABOVE This big-game
reel has a capacity of 450
yards (410m) of 80lb line
(36kg) to 220 yards (200m) of
150lb (68kg) line. It is fitted
with lugs for attachment to
the angler's harness.

LINES

By far the most common line for saltwater use is monofilament, along with the very similar looking multi-polymers. The minimum visibility provided by these lines has been enhanced by technological improvements that have provided extremely thin diameters per pound-test. Thus, smaller reels can be filled with the same yardage of a particular test that was formerly only used on a heavier model – this saves the angler both wear and tear on his arm and a few dollars. This has become most obvious in the big game area, where a drop of one size in a reel makes a big difference in price and may permit stand-up fishing with lines that were formerly considered strictly suitable for use by fishermen in fighting chairs. For instance, 50lb (22.6kg) big game reels, which are light enough for stand-up fishing, are now regularly used with 80lb (36kg) and even 100lb (45kg) thin monos for tunas that may run up to 300lb (136kg) or more.

It should be emphasized that every monofilament or multi-polymer line is a bundle of compromises. When too much of one desirable property is developed, you'll generally lose some of another. Thus, the angler should consider the type of fishing he is doing before selecting a line which is extra thin, or one which has a minimum of stretch, or another with excellent abrasion resistance. Colours are a matter of personal preference, though certain colours do seem to blend in better in various areas. Clear is safe, while pink, blue and green are often preferred.

Stretch is a problem inherent in monofilament and multi-polymers, but it also has some advantages. Though stretch is a disadvantage when jigging a lure or setting a hook, it also acts as a shock absorber, making it difficult to break the line at a distance even when mistakes are made. On the other hand, braided Dacron brings stretch down to about 10 per cent. This makes broken lines so common in the lighter classes that Dacron is not used much any more except for big game fishing. When a giant conger has to be pumped up, that lack of stretch is a big advantage. Dacron is also favoured for very deep-water bottom fishing. Braided nylon lines have just about disappeared from the saltwater scene, as they were both highly visible and extremely stretchy. Those casting with conventional reels were the last market for the limp and water-absorbent braided nylons, but they too have opted for monofilament in recent years.

Even the addition of lots of trolling weights to the above lines will not take them very deep when trolling. Wire lines cut through the water and bring your lure down about one foot for every 10ft (3m) of wire streamed. Thus, with 200ft (60m) of wire astern your lure should be working at about 20ft (6m). Monel is the most supple and least likely to kink of the wire lines, but slightly less expensive stainless steel will also do the job. Braided wire is easier to handle, but doesn't sink as well and can ruin rod rings. Lead core consists of a flexible lead strip encased in a sheath of Dacron or braided nylon. It is easy to handle, but quite bulky – and doesn't get down well in currents. Lead core is most suitable for relatively shallow situations.

Saltwater fly lines are heavier than those intended for freshwater use, and invariably feature a forward taper for maximum casting capabilities.

BELOW One of the essential qualities of sea tackle is that it should withstand corrosion from salt water. It should also be strong enough to resist the force of a reluctant catch, which may be as much as 10 times the weight of the angler!

Some companies even put out special saltwater tapers with slight modifications. Sinking lines are more commonly used than floaters, and a length of lead core may be added in special situations to attain necessary depths in currents.

Line quality is all-important, for at sea there may be a lot of line out; the tide may be strong and the fish stubborn. In a situation like this nylon can stretch considerably; better that it should, because without stretch it might give suddenly. The advantage of nylon is that for a given breaking strain its diameter is comparatively fine, which means that it offers less resistance to a tide-flow and enables the terminal tackle to get down faster. There are lines made of woven strands which do not stretch, giving immediate contact with fish. But the braided lines have a thicker diameter than nylon and because of the surface they offer more resistance to tide.

Sometimes a tide is so strong that more than the usual amount of weight is needed to get the baited hook down to the seabed. But the extra weight has also to be reeled back up to the surface, putting extra strain on rod and reel. Here, wire line can be considered but it has advantages and disadvantages. The main difficulty is that of kinking, for unless wire is kept very taut all the time it can develop kinks which will not come out, and wire is costly. The other problem is that taut wire is virtually a cutting instrument and it will prove it if the bare hand is used to grasp wire when the hook is snagged on the seabed.

As the boat rises on a wave the line does not stretch like nylon, and it will take fingers off in an instant. The good points? Wire is thin, offers little resistance to tide and is heavy, so less weight than usual is needed – and the pull of a biting fish is instantly felt by the angler. It is wise to connect the wire to the hook with a length of strong nylon; this gives slightly and avoids the possibility of the hook being pulled out of the fish at the first strike.

OTHER ITEMS OF TERMINAL TACKLE

The obvious difference between freshwater and sea fishing is the need for strength, reliability and corrosion-resistance in sea angling accessories. The best swivels are made in brass and of the type that do not allow sand and grit to abrade them. Buckle swivels, link swivels, and quick-release swivels allow rigs to be put together neatly and with confidence that not one of the items will fail. Booms of the two-eye Clement's and single-eyed Kilmore are sometimes fitted with ceramic-lined eyes but this does not seem to improve their performance to any degree.

Paternoster booms should be stout enough to cope with a fish's struggles without bending. An important point about hook droppers on paternosters: the length of nylon to the hook must be longer than the distance between each hook-length. This prevents any tangling of the hooks while they are on their way down to the bottom.

For heavy-duty work, sharking for instance, or large conger, it is better to crimp wire tackle. It is easier, safer and neater, and holds perfectly if the crimping is done properly.

WEIGHTS

For obvious reasons weights for sea fishing are almost always heavier than those used in freshwater, some considerably so. The names of the different kinds aptly reflect their shape and use: torpedo, barrel, coffin, bomb, grip, and spiral. Others need a little more definition. The Breakaway lead has wire arms that protrude from the side of the weight during

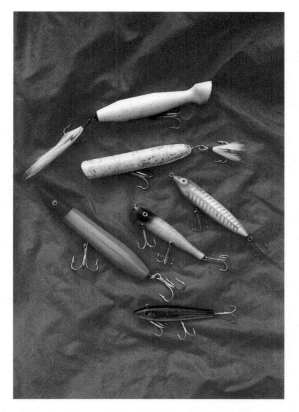

TOP Surface plugs of many types provide great sport.

ABOVE High-speed trolling lines come in many styles.

the cast and hold in the seabed. A haul on the line pulls the arms close and allows the tackle to be reeled in easily. Commercially sold weights are not cheap and many anglers dispense with them, using stones with holes or large metal nuts, all of which are expendable if tackle has to be pulled free when lodged.

LURES

There is such a diversity of saltwater lures, that it is impossible to separate many of them from freshwater models. Indeed, just about any freshwater lure will work somewhere and for something in the sea. As a general rule, saltwater lures are larger and heavier than freshwater models. Since the pace of life is much quicker in the ocean, retrieves are normally faster – and most lures are designed for such use. Especially notable as strictly oceanic lures are the high-speed offshore models; these lures are trolled at speeds of about 6 to 10 knots on average, and many will work at much greater speeds.

JIGS

Jigs of many types have been devised to work the depths for species ranging from tiny up to hundreds of pounds – and these are probably the single type of lure the author would want in his survival kit. The most common type of jig has a lead head and a hook dressed with bucktail, nylon or other materials. Another popular type is the diamond jig, a fast-sinking chromed-lead lure that may be rigged with just a single or treble hook – or with a tube tail.

Metal casting lures have flatter sides and can be used at all depths. Due to their shape, they don't sink as quickly as diamond jigs – though that can be an advantage in shallow waters. Most lures of this type are chrome-plated.

PLUGS

Saltwater plugs come in many sizes. Surface lures are the most fun, since the strike can be seen as well as felt. Swimming plugs are worked slowly and provide lots of action, while popping plugs are retrieved at high speed and will often stir up well-fed fish that would pass up more conventional lures.

FLIES

Saltwater flies are generally long and bushy compared with freshwater models. Rather than imitating specific insects and hatches as in trout fishing, the saltwater fly-fisherman simply must present something that looks edible – usually an imitation of a bait fish. Thus, the standard saltwater fly is a streamer, which can be anything from 1in (2.5cm) for small game fish to a 1ft (0.3m) creation. In shallow water, shrimp and crabs are the usual quarry for fish. Therefore, imitations of those crustaceans are most effective. In addition to the usual materials, saltwater fly-fishermen utilize a great deal of mylar and bright artificial hair. Larger, stronger hooks are utilized, and sink rates are often improved by using a heavier hook or adding lead to the hook shank.

BELOW Diamond jigs come in many variations, but all are designed to sink fast and produce a wide range of saltwater fish.

BOTTOM Bucktail and plastic-bodied lead-head jigs of many sizes are constant producers.

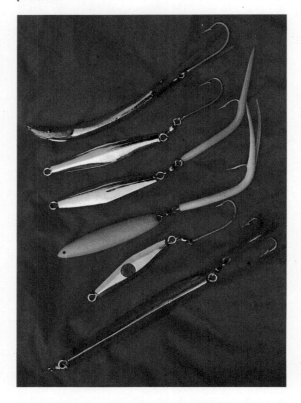

RIGHT This 1022lb (464.5kg) giant tuna was caught using a Penn 14/0 star drag Senator reel.

RIGHT A big coal fish caught from a deepwater wreck in New York Bight.

The Sea Angler's Fish Species

Compared with the freshwater angler, the sea-fisherman who goes afloat or fishes from the shore has many more fish species to try for. One kind of sea fish has bones of cartilage; the fish-shop standby 'rock salmon' will be known to many as the fish with the 'soft' bone running through it. Of course, this fish has nothing to do with salmon at all, but is a dogfish. The 'salmon' part of the name designed to appeal more to customers than the thought of eating shark.

SHARKS

There are very large shark to be caught in British waters. The world record for the porbeagle came from waters off Cornwall, a monster of 460lb (210kg). Another shark species common to British seas is the blue, with the mako making sporadic visits. Both of these reach well over 100lb (45kg), but the blue has suffered from over-fishing by greedy charter-boat skippers and many small specimens have been killed instead of being put back alive. The thresher shark uses its long, scythe-like caudal (tail) fin not only as a swimming aid but also to drive fodder-fish into groups before thrusting through them with its mouth at the ready.

The hammerhead is one of the real fishy oddities. It is difficult to see the reason for evolution producing a fish with protuberances either side of its head and eyes placed out on the ends. Head-on, these shark look like mobile range-finders. Marine biologists say that the eyed 'arms' also help in acting as wings for the shark's manoeuvres through the water.

A rare visitor to continental-shelf waters is the six-gilled shark but a small one of 9lb 8oz (4.3kg) was caught off Plymouth, Devon, in 1976 and is listed in the British records. It will not be the last of biggest six-gilled shark to be boated in British waters for much heavier specimens exist.

There are also basking shark. I have sat in a 16ft (5m) boat out off Coverack, Cornwall, while a group of 30ft (10m) long baskers cruised slowly round us. Not far off some of these vast creatures hurled themselves out of the water but luckily their playful games did not bring them near enough to swamp the boat. When the huge baskers fell back and hit the surface the noise and explosion of whitewater was like a depth-charge exploding. Basking sharks are, of course, quite harmless to man as they are plankton feeders, swimming just below the surface and hoovering huge numbers of these small crustaceans into their cavern-like mouths.

Between the large sharks and the lesser species is the tope, a fish which approaches 100lb (45kg) in weight and puts up a very doughty struggle when hooked on the correct tackle. This shark is one of the great sporting fishes for the light-tackle angler who knows just how to play the fish and just what his tackle can stand.

Other shark-type fishes are the lesser spotted and greater spotted dogfishes, the spurdog and the two similar smooth-hounds. The nasal flap structure of the two dogfishes is the most important and easily understood identification feature. In the lesser spotted these flaps are virtually joined, while in the greater spotted (also known as the huss or bull huss) the flaps are distinctly separate.

The main danger from these small sharks comes from handling the spurdog, which has a spine at the leading edge of each of the two dorsal

ABOVE The distinctive shape of the hammerhead cannot be confused with any other shark.

Blue sharks frequently swim right to boatside and stay there, waiting to be caught.

ABOVE A 405lb (184kg) mako shark goes up on the scales at Montauk Marine Basin at the end of the day. It was caught on a small game rod-and-reel with 30lb (13.6kg) mono after a 1¾ hour fight.

fins. All these fish provide good sport on the right kind of tackle, and this does not mean heavy-duty big-game rods and reels loaded with 100lb b.s. line. Only the heaviest porbeagles and very large conger need tackle of this kind.

One other shark-like relative, the monkfish, used to be caught fairly regularly in British waters, particularly quite close inshore at Westport, Ireland. But very few were put back alive due to their startling, male-volent appearance (good in photographs of the fearless angler with his 'trophy') and so their numbers dwindled, like so many species. Con-servation-minded anglers − *all* anglers, hopefully − should not fish for this species and if hooked they should be returned alive.

Related to the sharks by virtue of their cartilaginous bones are the skates and rays. These fishes have a 'flat' appearance but they are not flat-fishes in the sense that the plaice, turbot, flounder, and so on, are. They are ordinary 'round' fishes. There has always been some confusion about the difference between the skates and rays, the thornback at times being called both a skate and a ray. Both skates and rays are included in the family Rajidae, comprising about 30 species ranging from the very large common skate (another fish species becoming rare) to the much smaller species such as the cuckoo and spotted rays. All have patterns of prickles or spines on the upper surface, while a few carry them on the under surface.

The ray most commonly caught by anglers is the thornback, which reaches nearly 40lb (19kg). Some rays are comparatively rare and in many cases there can be problems in identification because the colora-tion, mottling patterns and eye-spots tend to appear to blend between the species.

The stingray and electric ray are ray-like fishes but are classified in different families, the torpedo ray in the Torpedinidae and the stingray in the Dasyatidae. Of the two the electric ray should be handled with extreme care for its name is an accurate description of the ability of this fish to produce shocks of between 10 and 220 volts, which are put to both defensive and aggressive use. When feeding it stuns the prey to quieten the fish before swallowing it.

Stingrays are not quite so properly named, for the serrated spines inflict deep wounds into which a venom is injected, but there is also the danger of secondary infection from bacteria on the spine. It used to be the custom for the spines of stingrays and spurdog to be cut off before the fish was released. This practice has largely died out, for to remove the defensive apparatus from any creature is to increase the odds against its ability to cope with its predators.

LEFT The long tail of the thresher distinguishes it from all other sharks.

ABOVE The spotted ray
can be confused with the
similarly-marked blonde ray,
but the upper wing markings
are a guide. The fish seen
here is a superb specimen of
7lb 9oz (3.4kg) caught off the
Devon coast.

ABOVE Legendary shark
expert Captain Frank
Mundus with the biggest fish
ever caught on rod-and-reel –
a 3,427lb (1,554kg) white
shark.

FAR LEFT A remarkable
catch of blonde rays taken
from deep water off
Lannacombe Bay on the
South Devon coast. The
species rarely comes inshore.

LEFT No doubt that
the tope is a shark, this
record fish of 58lb 2oz (26kg)
being caught by Ray White
from a North Devon shore in
1982.

ABOVE The rays are not attractive fishes, they have a kind of 'evil' appearance. The marbled wings of this 14lb 8oz (6.6kg) fish show it to be a small-eyed ray. It was caught off Start Point, Devon, by Terry Pooley.

LEFT A small but angry porbeagle comes over the side during a sharking trip off the coast of North Cornwall.

LEFT Down in the darkness of wrecks and reefs the ling waits for prey-fish to come by. This large, 38lb (17kg) specimen was tempted from the hulk of a wreck off the southwest coast.

RIGHT No fight, no glamour, but the lowly pouting is taken in numbers when the angler would prefer cod or pollack! Even a small pouting gives a hefty tug at the bait, which makes its appearance at the surface unwelcome.

THE COD FAMILY

Of the greatest importance to sea anglers are the cod family, which includes the cod itself, the pollack, coalfish or saithe, whiting, pouting, ling, torsk, haddock, some lesser species (the rocklings) and the blue whiting, also called the poutassou. This fish is appearing more and more on the fishmonger's slab because commercial trawling is decimating the cod. The hake is also a cod relative but it is notable in being more predatory than the others of its family: its array of sharp teeth testify to its habits. The hake is yet another fish which commercial fishing has put in danger through over-fishing. There are also two cod relatives of little or no concern to the anglers, the Norway pout and poor cod. Incidentally, there is one cod-type fish found in freshwater. It is the burbot, once living in the rivers of East Anglia but now extinct in Britain.

LEFT A beaten pollack comes to the surface, having accepted an orange lure fished deep. The large, solitary pollack can put up a strong initial fight, but they weaken quickly.

RIGHT Note the straight lateral line of this coalfish, it is one of the two identification points between it and the pollack, the other being the pollack's jutting lower jaw.

RIGHT There was excitement when this huge record-breaking conger was hauled over the side of Robin Potter's boat off Plymouth. It weighed 109lb 6oz (49.7kg) – and larger ones have been taken in trawlers' nets.

EELS

Both the silver (freshwater) eel and the much larger conger eel are found in British seas. The conger can grow to massive proportions which makes the sea angler's heart thump when he gets a bite on grounds where large congers are known to live. Thick as a wrestler's thigh and strong as a horse, a big conger is a formidable adversary when hooked anywhere where there are snags, such as reefs, wrecks or piles. Once it can wedge its body into a crevice the likelihood is that it will stay there, no matter how much pressure the angler can put on it. The way to cope with conger is to get them up into open water. At least then the angler has a chance of boating it, which is when the real fun starts!

LEFT Close-cousin to the turbot, the brill never reaches that flat-fish's weight. This very fine specimen brill was caught off one of the Channel Islands.

FLATFISHES

The true flatfishes (not the skates and rays, which have been briefly discussed earlier on in this section, and are 'round' fishes) are a group of fish which begin life as very ordinary fry, swimming the 'usual' way up and with their eyes in the usual place, one on each side of the head. But soon strange things begin to happen to the small flatties, one eye begins to move and migrate up and over the top of the head, ending up close to the other eye. The still very small fish then turns on one side and finishes its life swimming in that manner. Its coloration is also affected, the 'under' side usually becoming very white, while the side with both eyes develops brownish marking depending on its species.

Like the skates and rays, the flatties are bottom-living fish and include the turbot, brill, megrim, plaice, dab, flounder, and the soles. But there is one flatfish not yet mentioned, the halibut. This is a giant among the flatties: it reaches weights over 230lb (105kg), and is also predatory. Around Britain, the halibut is found in the deep, cold waters off northern Scotland.

RIGHT The flounder has an extremely wide tolerance of salinity. It is taken in pure sea-water, yet is also known to swim upstream for many miles into comparatively fresh water. This is the flounder record, weighing 5lb 3oz 10dr and was caught in the River Teign by W Burgess.

FAR RIGHT The turbot is a prime catch at any time. It is found on shell grit, sandy banks, but cannot be said to be widespread. The angler who brings a turbot home weighing 15lb or so will be forgiven all his sins.

ABOVE Anglers feathering for
mackerel will sometimes find
that a slender-beaked garfish
is on the line and is skittering
wildly across the surface
while being played. The
species often joins mackerel
shoals.

MACKEREL, TUNNY

The mackerel family is a very large group of fast, muscular fishes
characterized by a row of small finlets running from the dorsal fin and
anal fin towards the tail. The big-game aspect of sea fishing includes the
large, hard-fighting tunny and tuna, both members of this group of
fishes, but also the smaller and familiar mackerel. This fish has a dual
role in sea angling: it certainly holds its place as a remarkable tasty, oily
fish but is also a first-class bait for all other species, either whole or cut
into strips.

With the mackerel family in mind, there was for some years a considerable interest in the tunny before World War II when in 1933 a well-
known big-game fisherman, L. Mitchell-Henry, caught one off Whitby,
Yorkshire, which weighed 851lb (385kg). This fish is still the British
record for the species, but these large fishes seem to have moved away
from Britain's eastern coast.

While feathering for mackerel, it is not unusual for anglers to find that
they have hooked a garfish, the long, slender body of which glitters as it
leaps and dives to free itself. It is unusual in that when cooked its bones
turn green but it makes excellent eating nevertheless.

There is one small fish which has an even worse name than the
unwanted bootlace eel. It is the scad, or horse mackerel. There is something of a resemblance to the mackerel proper but it has no fight, no taste
and a multitude of small bones which just about sums this fish up.

OPPOSITE This big-eye tuna
must have wandered well off
course in 1985, for Andrew
Pascoe caught the 66lb 12oz
(30.3kg) British record while
fishing in Newlyn Harbour,
Cornwall.

OPEN *The* GUERNSEY BASS FESTIVAL

ABOVE Any bass weighing over 10lb (4.5kg) is a very worthy catch, so this fish, caught off Herm, Channel Isles, not only won an Open contest for its captor but also the admiration of his fellow competitors.

BASS

If one sea fish holds the same kind of admiration that the salmon has it is the handsome, strong and very edible bass. This fish can be caught in quite varied waters, from shallow estuaries out to the deep-water rocky pinnacles. Bass also tend to stay in shoals when young but become solitary in late adulthood.

There are some large natural harbours, Poole for instance, where numbers of small bass remain throughout the year, held by the water outflow from a power-station. These fish bear little resemblance to the large solitary bass which are found in deep, rough water in places such as the Eddystone Reef, Cornwall, and the Needles off the Isle of Wight. These silver, spiny-finned predators are fierce fighters when hooked on the right kind of tackle, and that is not the heavy-duty gear designed to haul ling up from the depths.

LEFT A fine 6lb 8oz (2.9kg) ballan wrasse caught at Salcombe by angling writer/ photographer/broad-caster Mike Millman. The ballan is easily the largest of the British wrasses.

WRASSE

Some of the most colourful of British sea fish species are found in the wrasse group. The largest of the species is the ballan wrasse, which reaches weights over 9lb (4kg). There are five or six species but only the ballan, the cuckoo and the corkwing have any interest for anglers. The British 'mini' fish record list shows how tiny the wrasses can be, for the Baillon's wrasse record is 1½oz (44g), the rock-cook's best weight approaches 3oz (85g), and the goldsinny's best recorded weight is just over 3oz (85g). All these fish are found in the vicinity of rocks. Few British fishes show major colour differences between the sexes. However, this occurs with the cuckoo wrasse. The male has a deep blue over much of the body and a white patch on the top of the head during the breeding season, while the female is a consistently brown overall.

RIGHT This is one of the reasons why the black bream's stocks have been badly hit. Small bream lie dead on a jetty after a 'bream contest'. With them are a very small pouting and whiting.

SEA BREAMS

The spiny-finned sea breams are a huge family of over 200 worldwide species although British waters hold but a few. These fishes are in no way related to the freshwater breams. The most common sea bream to anglers is the black bream which visits the South Coast of England in May each year to spawn over rocky reefs some 7 miles (11km) out.

It was once the delight of anglers to hold bream contests and so countless black bream were hooked, brought to the surface and boated – many before they had spawned. The roe of the bream is a delicacy and conservation was the last thing in any angler's mind. After all, the seabed was heaving with them! The anglers were wrong and bream numbers began to dwindle. The contests were stopped and it is to be hoped that this beautiful fish regains its former numbers.

Another sea bream, the red bream, is found in deeper water as is the gilthead. This fish was once quite rare but for some reason is becoming more and more common in British waters. The heaviest black and red breams weigh up to about 9lb (4kg).

RAY'S BREAM

The Ray's bream, again not related to any of the species named in the last two paragraphs, is named after the man who first saw it. This is occasionally taken by anglers but only up to a few pounds.

The bluemouth and Norway haddock look superficially like the sea breams, but are distantly related. They are occasionally caught by anglers fishing very deep water but do not reach more than a few pounds.

OPPOSITE This record-breaking gilthead bream weighed 9lb 8oz (4.3kg) when caught at Salcombe, Devon. Not a common species in British waters the gilthead is widespread throughout the Mediterranean.

RIGHT A fine thick-lipped grey mullet brought to the waiting landing net. Taken on freshwater tackle – note the bored bullet just above the hook eye – this is the largest of the four species of British mullet.

MULLET

To estuary and harbour fishermen the mullets comprise three fascinating species, the thick-lipped grey, the thin-lipped grey and the golden-grey mullet. They are all superficially similar, with detail differences. Mullet fishing is a sport only for the dedicated angler; the three are notoriously wary and light gear is necessary, even freshwater rods, lines, hooks and floats. While there are four 'mullets' on the fish lists only three are related, those described above and the red mullet which is a visitor from warmer Mediterranean waters.

GURNARDS

While there are four gurnards on the British record list only one, the yellow or tub, reaches any weight of note and that is 12lb (5.5kg) or so. These are fishes with armoured heads which at one angle can look almost cow-like. Their pectoral fin rays are thin and elongated and look finger-like as these fishes 'walk' about on the seabed. They also act as sensory organs. The gurnards should be considered as accidental rod and line catches.

WEEVERS

There are two weevers, one a shore-living fish, the other found deeper. Both are true venomous fishes, their dorsal fins and gill-covers carrying a strong poison which can inflict severe injury. The lesser weever lies hidden in the sand and bare feet can receive very painful stings, while the greater weever is sometimes hooked while boat fishing and again the unwary hand grasping this fish can get very badly poisoned.

OCCASIONAL VISITORS, TIDDLERS

The opah, sunfish, lumpsucker, and bogue all make sporadic visits and even more rarely are caught by anglers. But since they appear in the official record list their names are worth recording, as are the tiny blennies and gobies.

ABOVE Largest of the British gurnards, this tub, its large wing-shaped pectoral fins extended, was taken on a fine summer's day in deep blue water. A record-breaking tub weighed 12lb 3oz (5.5kg) when caught in Langland Bay, Wales.

ABOVE Prime, juicy lugworms ready to be sent down to the seabed for the attention of feeding cod. This is the red or 'blow' lug, but the larger black is preferred by anglers seeking cod or bass.

Sea Angling Baits

LUGWORM

No doubt, the ubiquitous lugworm is the sea angler's equivalent of the coarse fisherman's maggot. It can be obtained in large numbers, stays on the hook well and catches fish. In fact, for those living by the sea obtaining this bait is cheap and easy. A stroll along a beach at low tide where mud, sand and silt are mixed will reveal those tell-tale spiral coils beneath which the lugworm lives in a U-shaped borrow some 2ft (0.6m) down. This bait is one of a number of similar worms, and comes in lengths of between a few inches to 1ft (0.3m). Its colours depend on the substratum in which it lives. The one preferred by the angler is the black lug, which is supposed to have better fish-attracting abilities. It is hooked singly or as a bunch, or in 'cocktail' baits, a mixture of, say, lug and squid or other variations. I have known dedicated sea anglers to inject lugworm with pilchard oil before lowering the tackle over the side, but have no evidence that it increases the attractiveness of the worm.

RAGWORM

This is another marine worm of which there is more than one species. The kind found in harbours is smaller than the king rag which can be a formidable foot long. The king rag's earwig-like pincers can dig deep into the unwary finger. The ragworm is not a deep-sea animal, so its use as an angling bait is usually confined to beach-casting and other kinds of shore fishing. It stays alive well if kept in damp, wet seaweed. Like many invertebrate baits, if one dies the release of toxic elements soon kills others confined with it, so dead specimens should be taken out immediately.

ABOVE Another marine worm, but pincer-headed. The name rag covers a number of related species. Largest is the king rag, reaching 18in (45cm), found in coarse sand or muddy gravel, unlike the sand-living lug.

ABOVE There is no doubt about the value of fresh mackerel as a fish bait. Here, the tail and backbone have been removed, a large forged steel hook inserted and joined to nylon-covered wire line. This mackerel bait is intended for shark.

FISHBAITS

Here, a word about the treatment of all live baits. It has been known for skippers and anglers not to bother with the tiresome business of killing the fish quickly before taking the flanks off to produce a large bait. This practice is cruel in the extreme (whatever the theories about whether or not fish feel pain) and anyone seen doing it should be stopped and reprimanded in no uncertain terms. A good, hard crack on the top of the head quickly kills most fish, then the side can be cut off with a shark knife.

MACKEREL

All sea anglers will testify to the value of a fresh mackerel as the best possible bait. 'Fresh' means a mackerel which has been caught minutes before while the boat has paused in steaming out to the deeper marks. When a mackerel shoal is located they can be taken on six-feathered traces, six fish at a time, unhooked and kept alive in a container of sea water.

Whole dead mackerel make good shark baits and before being cast out their bodies should be pierced so that blood and juices can seep out to attract shark from long distances. When used as a conger bait, the head, with the entrails left hanging, is mounted on a suitably stout hook and fished on the bottom near a wreck or other conger-holding ground. When mackerel strip is used it is important that the glittering skin side be presented well as this is an excellent fish lure in itself.

LEFT Seen here, various ways of hooking dead sandeels including running the line through the lower jaw and nicking the hook into the belly.

HERRING

This species is becoming scarce due to 'trawler harvesting' and is hardly ever taken on rod and line and then purely by accident. Due to its scarcity, herring is not cheap and so few anglers will want to pay out a considerable sum for this very soft bait. It is not likely that fresh herring will be available to the ordinary angler unless he lives near the great northern trawler ports; as mackerel is just as good this fish is now preferable.

SMALL FISH SPECIES

Sprats can often be seen in fish-shops and these small, silvery fish make fine baits as whole fish for many species. The pilchard is a species that is not always present in British waters, but when available it can be put to the same uses as the sprat. Sandeels are sometimes collected by being netted in shallow waters, and they are one of the traditional bass baits. It has been suggested that whitebait also makes a suitable bait, but the author has little experience of this tiny fish on the hook. The bass will probably be the most likely species to be tempted by a little silvery whitebait on the right-sized hook.

ABOVE If there is one animal bait that fish prefer over all others it is peeler crab. This is the stage during which the crab's shell is soft and soon to be discarded, the new larger one, underneath ready to harden. With the old shell removed the crab is easy to mount and makes a very attractive bait.

CRAB

The crab most used as hookbait by the angler is the small shore crab, not the real heavyweight edible species. Like all crustaceans, crabs cannot just get bigger as they age and their armoured shell does not grow to accommodate the animal becoming larger inside it. When necessary the shell (properly known as the carapace) splits as the crab's body enlarges. In this state the crab is called a peeler. Then the shell is cast and the body is exposed making the creature vulnerable to all predators. It finds somewhere to hide until the new shell, which develops from its skin, hardens. It is now a soft-back. When the new shell has hardened, the crab, now called a hardback, can emerge and begin feeding.

Hermit crabs, those that make a home inside a gastropod shell, usually a whelk, make good baits. Of course, the crab, shell and all, is not put on the hook. The animal has to be removed. When freed (pulling is usually a waste of time, the result being a useless half of crab, so cracking the shell is necessary) the body is not crab-like, but still attracts hungry fish.

SMALL CRUSTACEANS

Prawns and shrimps make good small baits for float-fishing and if they are fished well down near fish-holding weeds and crevices they often attract bass or small pollack. The hook must be fine and inserted carefully into the tail segments so that the crustacean can wiggle and jerk attractively.

LEFT Squid is a natural food for many fish, so the angler can use it either on its own or as a 'cocktail' with lug. Most small squid offered as bait are from the Pacific, but now this cephlapod is accepted as food in Britain the indigenous squid is more available.

CEPHALOPODS

To the non-angler handling and mounting a small squid on a hook is as attractive as doing the same to a large black slug. But anglers are very quickly inured to any squeamishness of this sort, and anyway, squid make excellent baits for cod!

Tackle shops nowadays sell packets of small frozen squid. Those in the South West often obtain it fresh instead of the imported Pacific kind. The head as well as the tentacles stay well on the hook and when used with lugworm in a cocktail mix have taken many very large cod.

People who keep budgies and other pet birds will know all about the cuttle-bone that is poked between the bars of the cage to provide a supply of calcium. For anglers this 'bone', which is porous and is employed by the cephalopod as a buoyancy tank, is a nuisance, and must be removed. The cuttlefish also has a purple-brown outer skin which can be scraped off before the soft, firm white body can be used as bait. As with the squid, the tentacles used singly or in a bunch on the right-sized hook work very attractively in the current and fish cannot resist them.

ABOVE Limpets make
useful baits for fishes which
feed on rock-living animals.
Once firmly attached, they
are very difficult to remove,
but can be prised away with a
stout-bladed knife. The
muscular foot makes an ideal
hook attachment.

LIMPETS

Everyone who has scrambled round rock-pools and prodded – cautiously – under the weed-covered boulders there will be familiar with the limpets seemingly stuck fast, and the bunches of dangling mussels waiting for the next high tide. The limpets are being held by the strong, muscular foot which creates a vacuum to keep the shell firmly tight and the water in. A knife with a stout blade will dislodge them and the creature removed will provide excellent bait for flatfish, wrasse and shore feeders. The slipper limpet is a relative and can be used in like manner.

COCKLES

This is another bivalve which can be termed a 'perhaps' bait, to be used when the more standard offerings have failed. None of these baits are really suitable for deep-water fishing, for they are not naturally found except on the shore-line or close-in.

OPPOSITE TOP Like limpets,
mussels are good rock-fishing
baits. If left open for a while,
the body dries out and can be
mounted on the hook more
easily.

OPPOSITE BELOW Razorshell
(not fish) are more difficult to
obtain because they burrow
into wet sand and low-tide is
the only time when they can
be dug. On the hook,
razorfish is a prime bait for
flatfish and bass.

MUSSELS

The strong, thin thread that anchors these bivalves to their rocky platform is called the byssus. It is not permanent for the mussel can 'melt' it and move off, the animal excreting a fluid which forms a thread on contact with water and sticks firmly to the nearest rock. The mussel body is extracted in a similar fashion to the limpet, although the shell is not so difficult to open.

WHELKS

These large gastropods wander far and wide and are, like the crabs, the scavengers of the seabed. The shell has to be cracked to remove the body, which is a good bait for wrasse and flatfish.

RAZORSHELL

Sometimes called misleadingly 'razorfish' this long bivalve needs finding before collecting. Its discarded shells are often seen lying on the sand but living specimens are more difficult to obtain. Very often the small conical holes in the sand are clues, and a very quick thrust with a spade can reveal the unmistakable shape of this bait. Again, the fleshy 'foot' provides a safe hook-hold.

RIGHT The most famous of all sea angling artificials, these lures, colourful imitations of sandeels, have proved themselves time and again when fished over reefs and wrecks for cod, pollack, and coalfish.

PIRKS, RUBBER EELS AND SPINNERS

The pirk is a self-weighted metal lure that is lowered, then lifted sharply up and down, appearing to pollack and cod as small fish. They are remarkably efficient too. Small versions can be obtained which theory says will also take whiting and so on. The well-known rubber eel, which can be bought in green, red, brown and black is another classic lure which is worked round rock pinnacles and takes large pollack. Mackerel spinners take these splendid fish which pound-for-pound fight as hard as any fish in the sea. The traditional flounder spoon, too, works its magic, as the fluttering spoon makes just the same disturbance on the seabed as the small creatures eaten by this flattie.

GROUNDBAIT, CHUM, RUBBY-DUBBY

The amount of groundbaiting done by the coarse match-fisherman is not done in saltwater, although bread groundbait is useful when fishing for mullet. Chumming is an American term for throwing in quantities of chopped fish as an attractor. One member of the City of London Piscatorial Society surprised his fellow club members when he produced a huge bait-dropper or swim-feeder, very much like freshwater models (see photograph). But there is one attractor the sea angler employs which is a certain winner if there are shark within a mile or so. It is called rubby-dubby for some reason and the first time its presence is registered by the olfactory organ it will remain with the owner of the nose for the rest of his life. Even Trevor Housby, long-time shark fisherman and deep-sea angler of repute, calls rubby-dubby 'a revolting mixture . . . of many secret and highly offensive concoctions.'

The best mixture is old, smelly fish, preferably the oily species, fish offal, and pilchard oil all mashed up as finely as possible into a paste to which bran is added. This absorbs the oils and juices and the finer the particles the smaller the mesh of the vegetable sack in which the rubby-dubby is poured. Blood from chickens or oxen can be added, but the best blood, again according to Housby, is shark blood which sets the sharks into a feeding frenzy. When the rubby-dubby mixture is ready, Housby then leaves it 'to ripen in the sun for at least a day'!

In its fine-meshed sack, this noisome mixture is put into a plastic rubbish bin and carried (by those who can get near enough) to the boat. Keeping the lid on is advisable.

When the shark grounds are reached the sack is hung over the side. If the movement of the boat is not enough to knock the sack against the side as it hangs in the water, it should be prodded and thumped about so that oily particles stream out to form a slick which will move down-tide and bring the shark to the baited hooks hanging in it.

ABOVE Another huge sea-angling swim-feeder which when stuffed full of fish pieces would be lowered near to the baited hook. It was made by Morris Cleghorn, of the City of London Piscatorial Society.

TOP An adaptation from coarse-fishing methods: a trio of heavy bait-droppers for sea fishing. Home-made, they placed chum and fish-attracting goodies down near reefs and wrecks to bring pollack, coalfish, ling and cod close to the hookbait.

Off-shore Fishing

Sea fishing from a boat can be sub-divided into (a) dinghy fishing just off-shore and in harbours, (b) fishing from moderately sized boats with inboard engines and (c) deep-sea fishing from larger craft such as converted trawlers which spend 12 hours or more at sea. None of these kinds of boat fishing must be taken lightly, for one can drown just as easily in 8ft (2.5m) of water as in 100 fathoms. The sea is not particular.

Dinghies can hold perhaps two anglers, and should never be taken out so far from shore that in the event of a sudden squall shelter or beach cannot be reached quickly. Many have to be rowed, which cuts down the distance which can be covered, for rowing time means lost fishing time

ABOVE Netted launces – of the eels, however, it is the powerful conger which offers the most challenge for the sea angler.

TOP RIGHT Although the tub gurnard has been known to reach up to 12lb (5.5kg), as a rule, gurnards should be considered accidental catches.

RIGHT The fish most sought by sea anglers is the cod, not for its fighting qualities but because it is very acceptable for the table.

TOP LEFT Of the many species in the wrasse group, the largest is the ballan wrasse, and is therefore one of the few of interest to anglers.

ABOVE Wrasse caught off the southern coast of England.

LEFT The gilthead is one of the few bream found in British waters.

ABOVE Rather too many anglers on this charter boat speeding back to Guernsey after a day's fishing. Too many, perhaps, but they are all holding up good bass!

and that is not on for any angler. In any case, in many parts of the coast there is very good fishing no more than a few hundred yards out, especially where there are mussel or cockle beds. Codling (those cod up to 5lb (2.3kg) are usually known as codling) as well as bass come inshore to feed on these beds.

Sheltered waters of harbours sometimes make ideal fishing places and it is not always necessary to get out to the middle in a boat to catch fish. They tend to stay near walls, piles and any obstruction which would inhibit the free movement of vessels. There are some very large harbours and dinghies can be useful, but extra care has to be taken of the movement of other craft. As they manoeuvre they can quickly swamp small boats, especially when turning in confined spaces. Permission may be needed to go afloat in some harbours because of the dangers of boat movement.

The species found here will be mackerel, flounders, school bass, and small pollack. Light tackle is necessary because there will be very little depth, and the area will largely be sheltered from wind so the surface will not rough up. Float-fishing often makes entertaining fishing in harbours, especially for mullet, while the small bass can be sought by the use of bright, flashy spinners. Dinghy fishermen should not fish for large, powerful species such as conger, which also can be found among rocks and piles inside harbours.

Conger grow large on fish offal thrown into the sea by anglers gutting their catch before setting off for home. These formidable fish should not be gaffed and heaved over the side of a small boat, to thrash and writhe about round the feet of the captor, for it does not take a moment to lose

balance and upset the boat while trying to avoid the snapping jaws of an angry conger.

Very light tackle, small hooks and fish strip, or worm, can be used for harbour flounders, but the prime species must be the mullet. Here, float fishing, using bread paste as bait, can make for fascinating sport, but great care must be taken not to create too much disturbance, for the mullet is a wary and shy fish.

Every morning, summer and winter – and weather permitting – flotillas of charter-boats between 16 and 30ft (4.8–9m) long set out from marinas and ports all round the coast. These days all boats for hire have to be licenced. By and large the skippers are reliable men who know their part of the coast and have experience of where to fish in all the tide states and weather conditions. The usual number of anglers in these boats is four, with the professional skipper. If the boat is large enough he sometimes has a 'second in command' to do the work involved in anchoring, hauling in the anchor rope if there is no winch fitted, gaffing or netting fish, and making a welcome cup of something at least once during the hours at sea.

The skipper will have decided to head for a certain mark and if this is very popular he is usually accompanied by other boats. If the time of year suggests that mackerel shoals might be about he will head for likely areas (perhaps by watching for circling gulls or the smattering on the surface as the shoals work their way along). The skipper then stops the engine and the anglers set up strings of feathers so that a good supply of fresh bait can be collected before the serious bottom-fishing begins on a mark farther out.

ABOVE When the wind is making things difficult out to sea, many sheltered harbours and bays offer very entertaining fishing. These lads are fishing with light outfits for small inshore bass, mackerel, codling and so on.

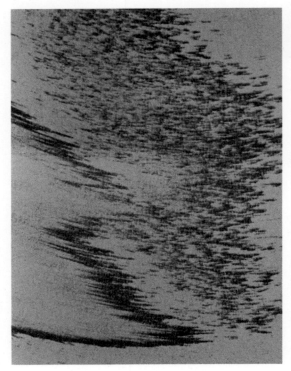

TOP Echo-sounders help anglers to locate likely fish-holding marks. Here, the boat is over rough ground, where fish will be found between the rocky pinnacles. Pollack will also hover just above the tops.

ABOVE When adjusted, echo-sounders can also reveal fish. The mottled trace above the jagged outline of the rocks shows that a shoal of bass are there.

The marks will be anything from half a mile to 14 miles (0.8 to 22km) and more out, but the time spent reaching the far marks is considered part of the day's hire, which means the farther out the mark the shorter the time for fishing before the 'Lines up!' order is given. Unless asked, skippers do not advise on rigs, baiting preparation and baiting up, methods, how to play a fish, and so on. But they, or the helper, will be ready with the net or gaff if the fish is too large to be lifted inboard. There is usually spare gear on board, rods, reel and made-up terminal tackle, but anglers almost always bring their own and have their own preferences for rigs. Some boats have fish wells into which the catch can be dropped to keep the deck clear. If conger come aboard this facility is very useful.

The normal means of sea fishing from anchored boats is to let down the tackle in the tide so that it streams out, the weight taking the tackle down to the bottom where it is ledgered, usually on a flowing trace. The weight is attached to a Kilmore or Clement's boom which is stopped on the line by a bead, the hook trace flowing out in the current. By raising the rod tip the weight can be lifted so that the hook-bait runs farther down-tide.

But many anglers prefer to cast up-tide from the boat, taking care not to snag the anchor rope. The advantage of this method is that it alleviates the danger of more than two lines becoming crossed and tangling down-tide, it places the bait in a position away from boat noise and the disturbance caused by the hull, and larger area of seabed is being fished. Up-tide casting has to have tackle that will hold when the weight touches bottom. Here a wired grip-lead is used and the hook length shortened to avoid snagging during the cast. This problem is not experienced when the trace is simply lowered over the stern.

The bigger craft, those capable of taking 10 or more anglers out to deep-water marks, wrecks, or reefs 20 miles (32km) or so out, will be at sea for longer periods and have some facilities such as bunks for resting, especially if the weather is rough and sea sickness begins to have its effect. The wreck marks are found by echo-sounders or more advanced fish-finders which give a clear picture of the seabed. These are often ships sunk in wartime or in storms and the finding of a 'new' wreck, one not so far logged by charter boat skippers, usually results in the catching of large numbers of very big conger, pollack and ling.

SALTWATER SPINNING

Freshwater one-handed spinning rigs will work just fine under many saltwater circumstances, though the marine angler generally prefers longer butts and one-piece models even when fishing with light tackle. Two-piece rods don't become common until lengths go beyond 7 or 8ft (2–2.4m). It is those longer rods and large reels which are usually referred to as saltwater spinning types.

Spinning differs from conventional fishing in that the open-face reel is used under the rod, and reeled with the weak hand so that the fish can be fought with the stronger hand on the rod. Saltwater spinning rods have long butts for two-handed casting, and generally utilize aluminium oxide or stainless steel guides. Boat and jetty models are those in the 7 to 8ft class which are suitable for the short casts made around jetties (where the fish are apt to be close to the rocks) or from a boat. Once again, there's no point in carrying around more weight than necessary – especially if you're casting all the time. Surf rods range from 8 to 12ft (2.4–3.6m) in one- and two-piece versions – and there are even a few up to 15ft (4.5m) in three pieces. Anglers casting lures opt for the shortest

RIGHT Trawlers can be hired
to take parties out for a day or
so and are able to steam out to
deep-water wrecks and reefs.
This boat is out from
Westport, Northern Ireland.
Sea conditions this far out can
demand that the anglers be
immune to the motions of a
gyrating, wallowing, slippery-
decked fishing platform.

ABOVE Saltwater
spinning reels are a popular
choice for many sea species
but perhaps have limited use
in British waters when their
cost is considered.

models practical for the job so as not to wear themselves out. The longer, heavier rods are most suitable for casting large baits and sinkers – and are often left stuck in a sand spike.

Spinning reels should be balanced to the rods, with medium spinners on 7 to 9ft (2–2.7m) rods and large-capacity models on those used for heavy-duty bait fishing in the surf or boat trolling and bottom fishing. Spinning reels are easy to cast, but have no advantage when it comes to trolling or bottom fishing. Indeed, their inherent lack of power mitigates against their use in those areas.

SALTWATER FLY FISHING

The basics of fly fishing don't change as you go from freshwater to saltwater, but there is a big difference in the tackle. The light wands used to cast tiny dry flies in streams have little application in the marine environment, and the simple single-action fly reels that are quite adequate for trout will not stand up to either saltwater or the larger, stronger fish which may be encountered. Specialized saltwater fly reels are quite expensive. Two models will also do the job for everything short of big game.

Drags are hardly a concern in most freshwater fly fishing, but they're very important at sea. An anti-reverse mechanism is also advisable when larger species are sought. The rods are generally longer and heavier, which enables the angler to cast large, wind-resistant flies a considerable distance. Nine-footers capable of handling forward-taper lines from number 8 to 13 are fairly standard in saltwater areas (even lead-core line is used in specialized cases), and they are normally equipped with short butt extensions that can be plugged in quickly in the act of fighting a fish. While graphite hasn't come to dominate in other saltwater rod types, it is generally the preferred fly-rod material with its combination of lightness and strength. The weight of saltwater fly outfits is a prime consideration, though few marine fly fishermen engage in blind casting.

ABOVE Surfcasting at
sundown; powerful
equipment ensures tackle is
cast over the breakers.

Fishing From The Shore

Most coastlines have a mixture of sandy beaches, shingle, mud flats,
rocks, cliffs, manmade harbours, and piers all of which need to be
fished in a way that allows the angler to get his baited hook to the fish,
play it without certainty of it being lost and get it ashore. This sounds
fairly obvious, but it does give an idea of the variety of shore fishing
round the British Isles.

From the beach, whether it is sand or shingle, the angler needs to cast
his tackle over the breakers so that his gear is not tossed back up by the
waves. This demands a powerful rod with a length which provides the
necessary impetus to the terminal tackle, sometimes 8oz (227g) or more
plus bait, swivels and so on. The layback style of beach-casting, developed by the late Leslie Moncrieff, allows the angler to build into his rod

ABOVE Ranks of
anglers often line the railings
of piers. When the tide is in,
there is often deep water
below them, so casting is not
necessary. But one good fish
could reduce all these lines to
one enormous tangle!

the power it needs to cast the terminal tackle to where the angler decides.
The art-work shows how this is accomplished.

Casting distance is achieved by rod and the weight of the tackle and a
formula can be used to show this. Rods will be between 10 and 14ft
(3–4.2m) and the weights and lines to match them run from 2oz (57g) and
12lb (5kg) b.s. line to 8oz (227g) and 15lb (6.8kg) line. Between line and
terminal tackle a length of strong nylon is used to take the initial strain of
the cast and this ranges from 18 to 50lb (8–22.6kg).

Multipliers are the best reels for beach-casting but there an element of
skill in timing must be acquired so that the thumb can come down on the
spool to stop lie running off at the exact moment that the tackle hits the
water. A split second too late and the dread bird's nest will appear as if
by magic. The result is temper and fishing time is lost.

Fishing from the many Victorian piers round the British coast is a
well-known holiday pastime but the occasional summer visit, with the

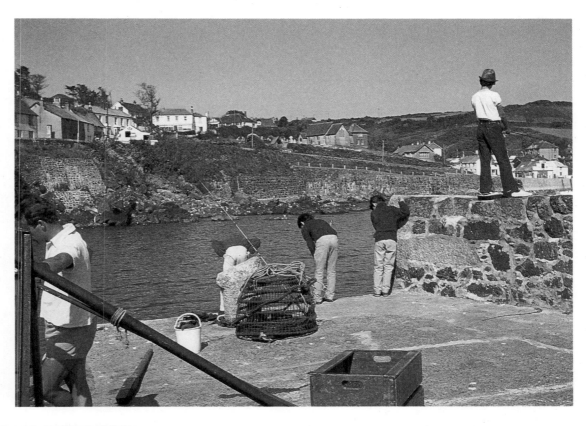

OPPOSITE The ultimate in rock-fishing! An angler casting from Pulpit Rock, Portland, Dorset. But bringing a fish up, even with a drop-net, might create a few problems!

RIGHT The small jetty at Coverack, Cornwall, where holiday-makers can try their luck with cheap tackle bought locally. There is something very special about these places, the fishing may not be anything to write home about, but the atmosphere is wonderful.

BELOW Piers are a prime site for fishing, although the dedicated fisherman is careful to avoid the crowds of summer visitors. This mullet was caught at Portland Harbour.

pier crowded with holiday-makers, children pounding up and down the walkways and the ear-splitting din from 'fun'-fairs is not the best time. The fisherman goes early morning before the crowds are up or in winter when the only visitors are anglers.

An advantage of piers is that when the tide is in the tackle can be lowered straight down without the angler trying to cast it to the horizon. Fish are more likely to be close or beneath the pier because of the continual fall of edible items dropped by visitors. The paternoster is probably the best pier rig, with the weight on the end of the line and the baited hook or hooks standing out on booms.

Everyone who fishes from a height such as a pier, harbour wall or rocky ledge must be equipped with a drop-net, for trying to wind even a 2lb (1kg) fish up, say, 15ft (4.5m) with a fixed-spool reel will put terrific strain on the bale-arm and spool as the tightly wound nylon is recovered.

Anglers should make enquiries about access before deciding to fish from a pier. Some authorities ban fishing altogether, some charge anglers a fishing fee and restrict the area from which they can operate.

Harbour walls can provide excellent fishing places, but they do not always have railings, so care should be taken when settling down to fish. A sudden strong pull can put an angler off balance. Drop-nets are a necessity here too. The Dover Breakwater is a famous fishing platform, although its official purpose is rather more than that! This venue, at the head of Dover Harbour, has seen catches of prime cod and other species. It is isolated, without a direct link to shore, so anglers have to make sure they have access and can return to shore at the end of the session. It is a place where food and drink as well as all-weather clothing are absolutely essential.

A rocky coast is always inviting to anglers. They know that the gullies between rocks can hold small crabs, mussels, whelks, shrimps and

ABOVE Action off the rocks!
Very often a helping hand is
most welcome when a heavy
fish has to be netted. A firm
foothold is absolutely essential.

marine worms all of which are taken by fish, so a baited hook is very likely to be snapped up by a small pollack or codling, even a bass. Rock fishing is fun and can be exciting, but danger lurks too. Weed-covered rocks are very slippery and in the excitement of a hooked fish the angler's balance can be minimal. One slip and – if nothing worse – a very wet angler. While the usual weather-proof clothing is needed, the kind of foot-wear essential must be studded, not smooth-rubber soled. The old familiar wellies will not do when standing on slippery rocks.

Spinning from a rocky platform is enjoyable. A fluttering, sparkling spinner worked through rock gullies can often bring lurking fish out to inspect and take it.

The shore does not have much of a reputation where big fish are concerned, but it can happen. One day in 1966 young Barry Jones was fishing from the beach at Tom's Point, Barry, Glamorgan. Then Barry's hook became snagged in the thick weed that lined the shore and he hauled and struggled to recover his terminal tackle which seemed not to want to be drawn closer. And suddenly Barry saw why. He had a cod on his hook which looked like a porpoise but he eventually got it ashore. When weighed it took the scales down to 44lb 8oz (20kg) – and that cod has held the British shore record for many a year.

LEFT A wrasse slides up wrack-covered rocks after being hooked on an inshore mark in the Channel Isles. For those not able to go out to sea without suffering from sea-sickness, rock and shore fishing offers very enjoyable sport.

LEFT Ground bait is a suitable lure for mullet; these wary fish demand patience and dedication.

RIGHT Casting in rocky areas is a challenge often amply rewarded, as fish search for food among the crevices.

BELOW Terry and Ian Pooley with a 13lb (6kg) blonde ray.

RIGHT The solitary pleasure of bass fishing from the shore.

Accessories

It is the author's experience that he can go afloat for a sea fishing trip carrying fewer 'bits and pieces' with him than when setting out for a day by the river. Assuming that the angler takes rod, reel, line, terminal tackle and bait with him, what else should he have in his fishing bag?

KNIFE

Every angler should have with him a good-quality, stout, sharp knife, with its own sheath. The knife will cut his bait, trim ends of nylon when making up rigs, and if the hook becomes totally snagged on the bottom it can cut the line to save the rod from damage. On the matter of bait-preparation, no skipper looks kindly on finding an angler happily carving away at a fish-bait while his knife cuts notches in the boat. A bait-board is usually available for this purpose, but some anglers have their own just in case. Diving knives that float are useful although if a tide is running past an anchored boat anything floating will be out of sight very quickly. For this reason, a tether that can be attached to knife and angler often saves much frustration and cost.

PLIERS

There is not likely to be the need for any electrical work to be done on board, but when hooks are firmly lodged in strong, bony jaws pliers are a boon. Some fish, large conger and shark, will also need the hooks removed and the unthinking angler trying to get a hook free with his fingers is liable to suffer a sudden bloody disaster. With conger, it is usual to cut the hook trace and drop the conger into a fish-well. Sharks are also being given different treatment. Today, conservation-minded anglers lash the fish close to the boat's side while the hook is removed, then allow the shark to swim off.

NETS AND GAFFS

Many anglers take their own nets with them, but not because they think the skipper will not have one. This is not unknown, but the skipper quickly finds that his customers go elsewhere). There can come a time when fish will be coming aboard all at once and the angler with his own net does not have to worry about losing a good fish while it is on the surface. Gaffs are going out of fashion for the small sea fish species, but there is usually one for large conger, for few men are strong – and brave – enough to coax a big conger into a net, then lift it aboard.

Gaffs are a very important item for big game fishing. Straight-handled gaffs with heavy hooks are fine for straight-pulling fish. However, flying gaffs are preferred for sharks (which spin). The hook of a flying gaff is separate from the handle, and is inserted into the handle for striking the fish – after which it pulls free and holds the quarry via a line attached to the boat. However, it is important to remember that the use of a harpoon is not allowed under IGFA sport fishing rules – a fish hit with one is disqualified both for record consideration and in any contest run under IGFA rules.

Gaffs are also important for smaller game, but the hooks are proportionally smaller and the handles only 3 to 5ft, (0.9–1.5m), rather than 8ft (2.4m) in length. The best bet is to have at least two aboard – one with a heavy hook that won't straighten out on large, powerful fish, and another with a light hook that penetrates easily into smaller fish.

ABOVE The deck of a boat is not the place to cut fish up. The baitboard in use here is ideal and can be part of an angler's accessories. It should be kept scrupulously clean, for a slip with a sharp knife as the boat rolls can inflict a wound letting in harmful bacteria.

OPPOSITE Adequate landing-nets are a must for all fishing places either on land or at sea. Without one here, the angler would be in some difficulty with the rail in the way.

LEFT Frank Mather demonstrates the use of the legs and body to fight a giant tuna – a technique that reduces the strain on the angler. Notice that he is not even using his left hand on the rod while reeling with his right.

HARNESSES

Big game anglers require a seat or kidney harness in order to be able to slide back-and-forth in a fighting chair. However, stand-up big game fishing is becoming ever more popular – and that calls for different equipment. Modern rod belts and kidney harnesses have made it possible to exert great pressure on a large fish with the short rods intended for this purpose – and without breaking your back in the process. The harness rests along the lower back and hips, and may be connected to the rod belt with drop straps so the rod pushes against the thighs rather than in the groin area, as they were formerly worn. Stand-up anglers may also use wrist bands and knee pads for added comfort while fighting fish weighing well over 100lb (45kg).

TACKLE AND FISH BOXES

Tackle boxes come in so many sizes and shapes that it is impossible to recommend a single kind of box for universal use at sea. Marine anglers should avoid any metal tackle box. Always obtain high-quality synthetic boxes and remember to check that the compartments are large enough to hold your fishing odds and ends as well as necessary items such as knives, pliers, hook hones and some kind of scales. Anglers' guesses about the weights of their fish are notorious for being economical with the truth. It is dangerous to leave fish inboard when they are coming over the side in numbers. The slipperiness of the catch combined with the roll of the boat can cause serious problems for anglers concentrating on playing their fish. Fish/bait boxes are always handy in these circumstances.

ABOVE The angler is pulled upright as his catch fights against a heavy drag. The harness is indispensable at such a time.

CLOTHING

Adequate clothing must always be taken aboard even if the day looks set fair and hot. If the boat is 15 miles out and it blows up wet and windy the angler either gets wet and fishes or hides in the wheelhouse, cursing. Waterproof clothing for sea use should be of the best quality, any leak through eyelets or down the neck results in an uncomfortable angler who cannot concentrate. Rubber boxes are not always required, for the angler will spend much of his time sitting and feet can become very hot in waders when the sun is shining. And the point should be made that waders will not be much use if the worst happens miles out! Rubber boots with studded soles should never be worn on board, they can scrape and gouge the deck planking. Best of all for cold-weather fishing is a working survival suit. Though quite expensive, these suits provide warmth and will keep one afloat should an accident occur. Furthermore, it is not necessary to wear foul-weather gear over survival suits.

There will come the day when the sun is hot, the sea calm and the wind a gentle zephyr. Off will come shirts and anglers will sit and cook slowly for hours. At the end of the day many will be sore and sorry, for sunburn is no more than self-inflicted injury and can be very serious. In the summer, carry some good sun oil or lotion to apply on bare flesh.

FOOD AND DRINK

I have a friend who has one major task to carry out before putting the fishing tackle on board his boat – 'essential supplies' which clink and rattle in their boxes. The various liquids in those bottles are enjoyable, in the correct surroundings and in modest quantities. At sea, before or after the sun has sunk below the yardarm, that kind of drink is not a good idea. The odd bottle of beer or can of lager (kept cool by hanging in a bag over the side) is hardly the epitome of evil, but thirst-quenching drinks are better. Real food, tea, coffee or cold drinks are the best. Do not expect the skipper to come round every few minutes with tea he has made, some do, some do not.

SEA SICKNESS

After food, one must face the fact that there are people who cannot go afloat without suffering this trauma. It can be beaten by some unfortunates after plenty of hard work in putting up with the unpleasantness for trip after trip. Even sea anglers are no different from ordinary humans. The author knew a very good, successful beach-angler who regularly returned home with a bag of fish. But the moment this unfortunate stepped on to the sand or shingle and saw the waves he was sea-sick! There are pills that are said to be infallible in warding off the dreaded pangs, but those who are liable usually suffer. What advice there is, is keep in the fresh air, try to remain standing, keep away from the diesel exhaust and the rubby-dubby bin! Never go to sea on an empty stomach, better to lose your breakfast than be seriously ill.

ON THE BEACH

Beach anglers often spend nights practising their sport. Some nights are fine and moonlit, but few are light enough for the angler to prepare rigs, cut bait up, bait hooks and so on. Tilley lamps are ideal and every beach angler needs one. Equally, he needs a large fisherman's umbrella, not necessarily for rain but to keep a chilling wind off. It is tiring and unnecessary to stand hour after hour holding a 14ft (4m) beach rod. Stout tripods and other rod-holding gadgets are available to do the job. And knife and pliers of course, are essentials.

CAMERA

The recording of some unusual event, or the capture of a specimen fish are reasons for having a camera in the fishing bag. But it is the experience of most anglers that they are playing the fish when the photograph should

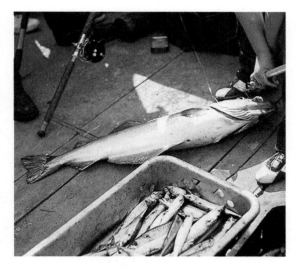

ABOVE Mundane, but good fishing practice. A stout fish-box helps to keep the deck clear of slippery baitfish when large pollock or cod are being reeled in to be unhooked.

be taken. One should have the camera ready (but, not, in the way or standing on the top of the cabin and getting salt-spray all over it) and come to an agreement with another angler or the skipper to use the camera when required. Make sure that the volunteer knows how to use it!

Big Game Fishing

The secret to success in big game fishing can be summed up in one word – technique. Very strong anglers are often able to overpower large game fish, but more often they're quickly reduced to a veritable bowl of jelly if they don't succeed in subduing their quarry quite quickly. This doesn't simply apply to people of average strength and years, but even those who are relatively young and work out regularly.

TECHNIQUE VERSUS STRENGTH

Some years ago I put Jerry Kramer, the famed ex-Green Bay Packer lineman, on a 150lb (68kg) class shark off Walker's Cay in the Bahamas during a Mako Marine Outdoor Writer's Tournament. Kramer, who is not only a big man but also a fine freshwater angler, tried to overpower the shark on 50lb (22.6kg) trolling tackle from a standing position. However, the shark didn't care for the sight of our boat and took off with a new charge of energy. Kramer had expended his power right away, and ended up having to hang on for a long time before I was finally able to get the wire leader and release the shark. That incident was not unique. I see it repeated time-and-again every year. In fact, most anglers who exhaust themselves quickly give up on the fish and pass the rod to a companion. On one occasion I had all three members of a fishing party on one yellowfin tuna of just a bit over 100lb (45kg) before the first one came back to finish the fight – which lasted only 20 minutes.

On the other hand, by employing the short-stroking technique (developed by West Coast, long-range party boat fishermen), a fellow fisher-

man of average size successfully wrestled each of six yellowfins – two of which were in the 100lb (45kg) class – to the anchored boat within five minutes. Outfitted with a 5½ft (1.7m) stand-up rod and modern kidney harness with a rod belt, he maintained constant pressure on the tuna as each short pump of the rod resulted in a few more inches of line on the reel. The idea is to avoid the long strokes that make it appear the angler is gaining a lot of line, but actually allow the fish to 'get its head' on each downstroke. The short pumps keep the tuna's head up and prevent it from diving to regain its strength.

THE STAND-UP FIGHT

Stand-up big game tackle and accessories have revolutionized the salt-water fishing world. After years of back-breaking effort while standing up with trolling rods, shoulder harnesses and belly rod belts, the toughest game fish can now be fought in relative comfort and with great efficiency. The 4ft 9in to 6ft (1.3 to 1.8m) fast taper, short-butted stand-up rods allow the angler to apply maximum pressure and lift the fish inch-by-inch as it circles below the boat.

Just about any tackle will do when a big game fish makes its initial run. With the fish away from the boat, you can snap into the harness and lean back on it while gaining a lot of line when the fish turns or the boat runs on it. However, even then (during the easiest portion of the fight) it is possible to wear yourself out. I've seen many fishermen wind the reel handle continuously as line is flying off the spool or the weight of the fish prohibits the retrieval of line. The effort involved in doing this will wear out anyone before the real fight begins, and will accomplish nothing.

The short-stroking technique comes into play when the quarry is straight up-and-down. At that point the angler must move the unwilling fish to the surface by the efficient application of pressure. Tuna circle continuously under the boat, and each circle provides the opportunity to raise the fish a few inches closer. Don't get caught with your rod tip way up in the air. Instead, concentrate on making short lifts – and be sure to start reeling before dropping the rod tip. All too often I see fishermen go through all the effort of lifting the rod tip, only to then drop it before they ever start reeling. The net result is a great deal of effort expended for no purpose – and such a fisherman will rarely make it through the fight unless he gets coordinated. It is hard to contain your enthusiasm when the biggest and strongest fish you've ever tangled with is pulling line off your reel, but by applying your strength selectively you'll be able both to enjoy the battle and complete it – rather than having to pass the rod over.

IN THE CHAIR

The same basics apply to a sit-down fight. Especially with heavy tackle, it is vital that you don't wear yourself out early. The fish must be fought with the back and legs – not the arms. By pushing back-and-forth in the chair, pressure can be applied and the fish moved so you can take a turn or more on the reel without even using your left arm to hold the rod. A bent butt, big game rod is an asset in most fighting chair situations as it allows for more efficient pumping.

A technique I've found to be very valuable in dealing with giant tuna when double lines are used is to utilize a gloved hand on the double line once it is on the spool. This extra pressure should roll the tuna over and prevent it from getting its head to make another run. The double gives you twice the breaking strength you've been fighting the fish with, and

ABOVE This superb specimen, a blonde ray, weighed in at 28lb 8oz (13kg).

OPPOSITE BELOW Once common in British waters, the blue shark's numbers have been diminished through over fishing.

LEFT Party boat fishermen with the bass and brill caught off the Channel Islands.

BELOW Dawn is the perfect time to troll for big striped bass when the tide is right.

any tuna which is still fresh should be taken right then and there before it regains its strength and takes off again.

The boat does most of the work in the course of fighting a big game fish from a chair, but the angler is called on to do more from a small boat. With the fighting chair mounted in the bow, the ideal situation is for the fish to tow the boat and tire itself out. However, giant tuna eventually find there's less pressure when they stay directly below the boat. That is when the angler must really go to work. Most small-boat chairs have no foot rests, and the angler uses the inside of the gunwale to obtain a purchase for pumping the fish up. With the chair in the bow, the skipper keeps track of the fight while looking forward, and can easily hold the fish away from the props and trim tabs at the stern.

PARTY BOAT FISHING

Charter-boat anglers must make some adjustments in order to fight big game fish. Movement is a must, particularly when the boat is anchored – which is usually the case. The idea, just as with smaller game, is to move with the fish so as to keep it directly in front of you. By doing that, you'll be able to avoid a cut-off should the quarry make a sudden move in any direction and you'll also usually prevent tangling with other anglers' lines. When a fish suddenly makes a run from bow to stern or vice-versa, the angler or crew members should take the rod by the end of the butt, point it straight down, and run from one point to the other. It is important for anglers to release the reel from harness straps at boatside in order to make the last minute moves with the rod tip necessary to prevent loss under the boat. Fish are moved to one corner of the stern or the other in

ABOVE Party boat anglers with cod, pollack and white hake.

ABOVE Working birds are a sure sign that game fish are below.

order to avoid tangling with the props and rudder in the middle. The most critical moves in party boat big game fishing involve getting the rod under the anchor line when the fish circles the bow. This invariably involves at least two people, one to hold the rod under the taut line and the other to get a firm grip on it from the opposite side. The basic rules apply to charter-boat fishing in general. Always follow your fish in order to avoid most of the tangles which are a prime headache in this sport. Light tackle is great sport and often more effective in hooking fish, but the charter-boat fisherman must use some reason in deciding what can be used under the circumstances. What may be appropriate with a small week-day party may not be reasonable on a crowded weekend.

While small boat anglers can usually avoid being stripped by an unexpectedly big fish simply by buoying their anchor line and drifting or running after the fish, the shore and pier fisherman is much more restricted. Therefore, he must be sure that his reel capacity is sufficient for the fish he may encounter. Surfcasters regularly try to cast to the horizon, but fish are often feeding right in the breakers and that area should not be overlooked. Even more so, those working piers and jetties should spend much of their time casting alongside the rocks which are a natural attraction for many game and bottom fish.

Light-tackle fishermen should learn from their big-game brethren and utilize a pumping technique when working in large fish – and those using spinning tackle must take special care not to turn the reel handle when line is going out or none is being retrieved. Whereas the latter merely saps strength when using revolving spool reels, on spinning reels every turn of the handle under such circumstances puts a twist in the monofilament. After a while, the line becomes so twisted as to be virtually unusable until straightened out. This can be accomplished by cutting off all terminal tackle and running the line out astern of a moving boat.

SETTING THE DRAG

One important point that applies to all fishing involves the drag. Drags are best set with a good spring scale. The true test of drag is off the rod tip, not directly from the reel, and most fishermen will probably find that their drags are set too light when they actually test them. As a general rule, set your strike position at about 20 per cent of line breaking strength, and push that up to 33 per cent for full drag.

Set your drag before you start fishing, and then stick with it. For some reason, many saltwater fishermen panic when they watch line being pulled off their reel. Instead of holding the rod high and making the fish use maximum energy in the course of that run, they instinctively screw down the drag to stop the run. Not surprisingly, that sudden shock in stopping a fast-running fish frequently results in a broken line. You would almost believe that some people figure the reel is filled with line just so there will be some left when they screw down the drag and break off!

Incrasing drag is something you generally do not want to do, because drag automatically increases as the amount of line on the spool decreases. Though there are times you'll want to add pressure, it is better to do it with your hands rather than the reel. Finger pressure can be applied lightly to the spool or to the line against the foam or cork foregrip of the rod. That added pressure is often necessary in order to pump up a big fish. The sheer weight of the fish may pull line from the reel, and all your pumping could be for naught unless you prevent that with some finger pressure.

ANALYZING FISHING CONDITIONS

The saltwater angler must deal with even more variables than his fresh-water counterpart. Though all of us are frustrated by situations where conditions are perfect but the fish still do not cooperate, the successful fisherman is usually one who takes all the natural factors into account and puts himself in the right place, at the right time.

WEATHER, TIDES AND CURRENTS

Weather is one of the prime variables. It determines both where and whether we'll be fishing, and has a similar powerful influence on the fish we seek. For instance, a storm featuring large ground swells may ruin inshore bottom fishing in ocean areas for days thereafter due to turbidity on the bottom – but surface feeders could go on a rampage under the same conditions. It will take a while before you become familiar with weather effects in your area, but that knowledge will save some wasted trips.

Tidal movements over high spots on the bottom are a powerful fish attraction, and there is usually some indication on the surface as to the existence of some kind of structure below. In shallower areas, a rip line forms on the surface when the tide is running – particularly when the wind is blowing against the current. Predators gather at the base of the rip to bait fish being swept over the structure, and anglers can troll lures at that edge (usually with wire line to bring the lure to the feeding depth) or fish it with jigs by drifting across or by stemming the tide and dropping jigs back into the pay-off zone.

The surfcaster must be particularly aware of what lies before him. A blind cast may leave his bait sitting on a bar in water too shallow to attract game fish. Check the beach out at low tide so you can determine where the various gaps in the bars are, and then fish those gaps (which are natural passageways for game fish) on the higher tides. Soon you will be able to analyze wave movement to determine where the deeper spots are.

Always keep your ears open while on the water. An unseen splash may lead you to a concentration of fish. I've fished quiet bays and creeks on many dark nights when my primary clue as to where to cast a lure was the sound of a splash or swirl.

BIRD CLUES

One of the most obvious clues to sight is bird action. It takes some experience to tell the difference between birds looking and birds working, but you'll soon get the hang of it. Birds diving on the water usually signal the presence of fish below, though there are occasions (particularly on slack water) when schools of fish will rise to the surface and provide easy pickings despite a lack of feeding predators. Even birds sitting on the water can be a clue to future activity: they may be hanging around bait fish, and there could be action when some condition changes. Ordinarily, you'll be looking for flocks of birds. However, a single bird may spot a fish close by before the others zero in.

A FEEL FOR ROD AND LINE

All of the foregoing becomes part of acquiring a feel for fishing. The rod in your hand should become a part of your body, and what you feel through it will determine how a lure must be worked – or whether there's still bait on your bottom rig. Successful bottom fishing and jigging

BELOW The wrong combination of wind, swell and tide can make even safe inlets risky for boaters.

ABOVE The charter-boat guide ensures the safety of anglers who are perhaps less experienced sailors. Any off-shore fishing should be attempted with caution as even the calmest water can be treacherous.

requires that you have a good feel of bottom. Fishermen who can't feel the slacking as a jig or weight hits bottom, and can't get the hang of maintaining a tight line contact with bottom as they drop back in response to the current, will not do well in the sport. I always keep my fingers on the line to feel anything which would give me an indication of what might be going on below.

Though rods are normally placed in holders for trolling, I usually hold my rod while trolling inshore waters – particularly with wire line. This enables me to get a feel for how the lure should be working, and I can compensate in boat speed for variations in the currents throughout the tide. Furthermore, I'll know if I hit bottom and must shorten up, or if I've picked up a bit of weed that will make the lure ineffective. Best of all, I'll be able to feel the slightest bump on the lure.

The sense of feel is particularly vital if casting lures. You must acquire the touch in retrieving lures at the correct rate both for the type of lure under the circumstances and for the species you're seeking. On a dark night you may have nothing to work with but your sense of feel in determining whether your lure is working correctly. Some fish, such as the mackerel, require a fast retrieve while others prefer a slow-moving lure. By varying your retrieve, it may be possible to pick out more desirable species with the same lure in a given area.

RECORD KEEPING

Something that has worked well for me and should be copied by every angler is record keeping. Being able to refer to records of every fishing trip over the years will provide information that can make you a better angler. Perhaps more important than that is the opportunity to re-live memories of trips – with all the details correctly stated. Record keeping will also enable you to compete against yourself. In this age of big money fishing tournaments, there is a lot of controversy about their effect on the sport. However, regardless of your feelings about competitive fishing,

ABOVE Electronics permit experienced boaters to fish offshore in even thick fog – providing catches such as this giant tuna caught off Block Island, Rhode Island, US.

RIGHT A fine catch of pollack from the English Channel.

there can be nothing but pleasure involved in trying to outdo yourself in catching the biggest and the greatest number (hopefully released) over the years. There is no need for a fancy journal (a simple notebook will do), and you will soon find that it is easy to keep track of the catch in your head during a day of fishing. Carry an accurate scale with you at all times, so even released fish can be weighed.

By combining the use of all your senses along with a knowledge of the conditions and the species sought, you can be among the 10 per cent of saltwater fishermen who catch 90 per cent of the fish!

Tides and currents are vital factors in saltwater fishing. Most species feed when there is a current running but shut off in slack water. However, there are many exceptions to that rule, particularly in bottom fishing when currents are strong. On any given day, certain species may hit on one tide but not the other. Usually this relates to bait movements, but there are occasions when bait is abundant on both tides while game fish feed on only one. Currents are equally important far offshore, where a shift can bring in warmer or cooler water and either help or hinder angling. Offshoots of the Gulf Stream, called eddies, often provide outstanding fishing in the canyons of the north-east. The rise and fall of the tides changes the nature of inshore fishing grounds. Prime high tide spots may be too shallow, or even out of water, on low tide. The greater rise and fall of the tide around the full and new moons has a profound effect on fishing. Currents will be stronger at these periods, and fish may react in various ways.

USING YOUR SENSES

The key to successful saltwater fishing involves bringing all your senses into play. Sight is obviously an important sense, as in almost every type of saltwater fishing there are visual clues that can lead you to better sport simply by observing and understanding them.

ABOVE A large bass caught off Alderney.

LEFT The cod family includes a species of great interest to the sea angler, like this 26lb (11.8kg) coalfish.

INDEX

Italic page numbers refer to illustrations

A

Ace of Spades lure *119*
Adams fly *134*
Anglers' box 58, *58*
Appetizer lure *122*

B

Baby Doll lure *122*
Bait-droppers 62
Bait-stands 62
Bait-trays *61*
Baits: animal *55*, 56
  barley 55
  bloodworms 52
  bread *52*, 53
  bread flake 54
  bread paste 54
  breadpunch 54
  casters 51
  caterpillars 52
  cephalopods 173, *173*
  cheese 54–5
  coarse fishing *46*, 50–7
  crust 54
  crustaceans 172, *172*
  deadbaits 57
  fishbaits 57, 170–3, *171*
  herring 171
  high-protein 56
  livebaits 57
  lugworms 168, *168*
  mackerel 160, 170, *170*
  maggots *50*, 51
  mealworms 52
  meats 56
  minnows *55*
  mussels *46*
  plants and fruits 56–7
  ragworms 169, *169*
  rice 55
  sea fishing 160, 168–77
  seeds 55
  shellfish 174–5, *174*, *175*
  slugs 10, 53, *53*
  sweetcorn 55
  tares 55
  vegetables 55–6
  wheat 55
  worms 52–3
Barbel 28, *28*
Barley bait 55
Bass 162, *162*, 171, 180, *180*, 188, *191*, *203*
Bibio fly *113*
Big game fishing 196–203
Bite indicators 38, 40, *40*, 42, 62
Black Bivisible fly *133*
Black Ghost lure *120*
Black Gnat fly *133*
Black Marabou Muddler lure *119*
Black Nymph *124*
Black and Orange Marabou lure *118*
Black and Peacock Spider fly 106, *106*, *107*, 108, *108*
Black Pennell fly *114*
Bleak 35
  as bait 57
Blennies 167
Blood knot *76*, 77
Bloodworms as bait 52
Blue Charm lure *121*
Blue Pheasant Tail fly *135*
Blue whiting 154
Blue Winged Olive fly *134*
Bobbin holder 98–9
Bogue 167
Bread bait *52*, 53, 54, 177
Bream 28
  as bait 57
  black sea bream 164, *164*
  gilthead sea bream 164, *165*, *179*
  Ray's sea bream 164
  red sea bream 164
Brill 157, *157*
Bullhead as bait 57
Burbot 154
Butcher fly *115*

C

Carp 27, *27*
  common *37*
  crucian 27
  mirror *37*
Cased Caddis nymph *126*
Cast connectors 76
Casters as bait 51–2
Catapults 60, *61*, *62*
Caterpillars as bait 52
Cephalopods as bait 173, *173*
Charr 81
Cheese bait 54–5
Chinook 82, *82*
Chub 10, 29, *29*
Chumming 177, *177*
Cinnamon and Gold fly *115*
Cinnamon Sedge fly *130*
Clubs and societies 20–1
Coalfish *148*, 154, *155*
Coarse fishing 14–15, 16–63
  accessories 58, *58*, *59*, 60–3, *60*, *61*, *62*, *63*
  baits *46*, 50–7
  clubs and societies 20–1
  float fishing 38–40, *38*, *39*, 58, *58*
  float-legering 42
  hooks 22, 24
  landing-net 44
  legering 40, *41*, 42
  lines 22
  lures 42, 44
  matchfishing 24–5, *24*
  playing a fish 44
  reels 22, 42
  rods 21–2
  species 26–35
  specimen hunting 19
  spinning 42, 44
  waters 44, *44*, *45*, 46, *47*, *48*, *49*, 50
  weights 38–9, 40, 42
Cockwills Red Brown nymph *126*
Cod *12*, 15, 154, 177, *178*, 180, 188, *199*, *203*
Colonel's Creeper nymph *127*
Conger eel 150, 156, *156*, *178*, 180–1
Conservation 12, *12*, 14
Cove knot *76*, *76*
Crayfish as bait 56
Crust bait 54
Crustaceans as bait 172, *172*

D

Dab *13*, 157
Dace 29
Daddy Long Legs (Crane Fly) *130*
Damsel Nymph *124*
Dark Hendrickson fly *133*

Daves Sculpin lure *119*
Disgorgers 58, 60
Dog Nobbler lure *119*
Dogfish 149
Double-haul castings 79
Dry flies 96, *98*, 99, 111
Dubbing needle 99
Dubbing twister 109, *109*
Dunkeld fly *115*
Durham Ranger fly *104*

E

Echo-sounders 182, *182*
Eels 150, 156, *156*, *178*, 180–1
Electric ray 150
Elk Hair Hopper fly *131*
Elvers as bait 57

F

Fish baits 57
Fish-finders 182
Flatfishes 157
Flies: fly fishing 70, *see also* fly tying
    sea fishing 146
Flies as bait 56
Float fishing 38–40, *38*, *39*, 58, *58*
Float-legering 42
Floaters *66*
Flounder 157, *158*, 180, 181
Fly fishing 64–135
    backing 69, 74
    cast connectors 76
    casting 77–80
    flies and fly boxes *69*, 70, 95–135, *see
        also* Fly tying
    grease and sinking agents 70, *71*
    hooks 100–1, *101*
    knots and loops *74*, *75*, 76, 77
    landing nets *71*
    leaders and tippets 69–70, *69*, 74, *74*,
        76, 79
    lines 65, *66*, 67, 68, *74*
    reels 68–9, *68*, 74
    rivers and lakes 73
    rod rings (guides) 66, *67*, 76–7
    rods 66–7
    sea fishing 73, 146, 183
    shooting heads 67
    species 81–2
    streams and ponds 72
    tackle 65–73, *66*
    waters 83–93
Fly tying 95–135

dope 108, *108*
dry flies 96, *98*, 99, 111, 130–5
feathers 108, *109*, *110*
flashabou 108
hair and fur 108
hare's mask 108
hen hackles 106, *107*, 108
hooks 100–1, *101*
leeches 100
lures 97, 100, *100*, 117–22
marabou plumes 108
materials 105, 106, 108–9, *110*
Matuka 100, *100*, 118
Muddler 100, *100*, 117, 119
nobblers 100, *119*
nymphs 96, *98*, 99, 124–8
ostrich herl 108
peacock herl 105, *105*
proportions 99–101
standard wets 97, 99–100, *99*, 105–6,
    111–15
streamer pattern 100
techniques 101–8, *102*, *103*; *104*, *105*,
    106, *107*, *108*
tinsels 108
tools 97–9, 109
French Partridge Mayfly *130*

G

Gaffs 192
Gallows tool 109, *109*
Gobies 167
Gold Ribbed Hare's Ear nymph *125*
Golden Shrimp nymph *128*
Grayling 31, *31*, 65
Green Bitch Creek Nymph *126*
Green Chomper nymph *128*
Green Thorax PTN *127*
Greenwells Glory fly *115*
Grey Duster fly *135*
Gudgeon 35
    as bait 57
Guides *see* rod rings
Gurnard 167, *167*
    tub 167, *167*, *178*

H

Hackle pliers *97*, *98*
Haddock 154
Hair stacker 109
Hake 154, *199*
Halibut 157
Herring 12
    as bait 171

Hook sharpener 62–3
Hooks 22, 24, 100–1, *101*

I

Invicta fly *112*

J

Jardine snap-tackle 56
Jersey Herd lure *117*
Jigs, sea fishing 146, *146*

K

Keep-nets 60–1

L

Landing-net 58, *59*
    coarse fishing 44
    fly fishing *71*
    sea fishing 192, *192*
Lead Bug nymph *127*
Leaders 69–70, *69*, 74, *74*, 76, 79
Leeches 100
Legering (ledgering) 40, *41*, 42
    float-legering 42
Light Cahill fly *131*
Light Cahill nymph *128*
Light Spruce lure *117*
Lines: coarse fishing 22
    fly fishing 65, *66*, 67, 68, *74*
    sea fishing *141*, 143–5, *145*
Ling 154
Loop-to-loop knot *75*
Lugworm bait 168, *168*
Lumpsucker 167
Lunns Particular fly *135*
Lures: coarse fishing 42, 44
    fly fishing 97, 100, *100*, 117–22
    sea fishing 146, *176*, 177

M

Mackerel 160, *160*, 180
    as bait 160, 170, *170*
Maggots as bait *46*, 51
Mallard and Claret fly *113*
Marrow spoon 70, *70*
Matuka fly 100, *100*, 118
Mealworms as bait 52

Meat baits 56
Megrim 157
Micky Finn lure *120*
Minnow 35
   as bait *55*, 57
Mirror carp *36*
Monkfish 150
Montana nymph *125*
Mrs Simpson lure *118*
Muddler 100, *100, 117, 119*
Muddler Minnow lure 100, *100, 117*
Mullet 166, 180, 181, *190*
   golden-grey 166
   red 166
   thick-lipped grey 166, *166*
   thin-lipped grey 166
Multipliers: coarse fishing 42
   sea fishing *141*, 142, *142*, 185
Munro Killer lure *121*
Mussels as bait 56

N

Nail knot 75
Needle knot *74*, 76
Nobblers 100, *119*
Nymphs 96, *98*, 99, 124–8

O

Olive Elk Wing Caddis fly *135*
Opah 167
Overhead cast 78–9, *78*

P

Palomar hitch *75*, 77
Pennell rig 57
Perch 35, *35*
Peter Ross fly *112*
Pike *10*, 34, *34*
Pirk lure 177
Plaice 157
Plugs: coarse fishing 42, *42*
   sea fishing *145*, 146, *146*
Plummet 63
Pollack *12*, 15, *140*, 154, *155*, 177, 180,
   188, *199, 202*
Pollution 12, 39
Polystickle lure *121*
Poutassou 154
Pouting 154, *154*
'Pressure of fishing' 38
Prey-fish *154*
Priest 70, *70*

Prince nymph *125*
PVC Nymph *124*

Q

Quill Gordon fly *134*

R

Ragworm bait 169, *169*
Ray 150
   blond *152, 190, 197*
   cuckoo 150
   electric 150
   small-eyed *153*
   spotted 150, *152*
   stingray 150
   thornback 150
Record keeping 202–3
Reels: coarse fishing 22, 42
   float fishing 40
   fly fishing 68–9, *68*, 74
   sea fishing *139*, 140, *140, 141*, 142,
     143, 182–3, *183*
Rice bait 55
Richard Walker Sedge fly *133*
Roach 32, *32*
   as bait 57
Rocklings 154
Rod rings: fly fishing 66, *67*, 76–7
   sea fishing 140
Rods: coarse fishing 21–2
   float fishing 39
   fly fishing 66–7
   rod-rests 61–2
   sea fishing 138, *139*, 140, 182–3, 185
Roll cast 77, 78
Royal Coachman Bucktail lure *122*
Royal Wulff fly *130*
Rubber eels 177
Rubby-dubby 177
Rudd 30, *30*

S

Saith 154
Salmon: Atlantic 82
   king (spring) 82, *82*
   Pacific 82
Scad 160
Scales *62*, 63, *63*
Scissors, fly tying 98, 109
Sea fishing 15, 137–203
   accessories 192–6
   big game fishing 196–203
   booms 145

chumming 177, *177*
drag, setting 200
echo-sounders 182, *182*
fish-finders 182
fishing conditions 201
fly fishing 73, 146, 183
from the shore 184–91
gaffs 192
groundbait 177
harnesses 194, *194*
jigs 146, *146*
line *141*, 143–5, *145*
lures 146, *176*, 177
multipliers *141*, 142, *142*, 185
nets 192, *193*
off-shore fishing 177–83
plugs *145*, 146, *146*
reels *139*, 140, *140*, 142, *143*, 182–3,
   183
rod rings (guides) 140
rods 138, *139*, 140, 182–3, 185
rubby-dubby 177
species 149–67
spinning 177, 182–3, *183*
swivels 145
tackle 138–48, 184–5
trolling 144, *145*
weights 144, 145–6
Seed baits 55
Sewn and whipped loop 75
Shark *14*, 15, 149–50
   basking 149
   blue 149, *150, 198*
   hammerhead 149, *149*
   mako 149, *150*
   porbeagle 149, 150, *153*
   thresher 149, *151*
   tope 149, *152*
Shellfish as bait 174–5, *174, 175*
Shooting heads 67
Shrimps as bait 56
Side cast 79, *80*
Silver Darter lure *117*
Silver Invicta fly *114*
Single-haul castings 79
Sink-tips *66*
Sinkers *66*
Skate 150
Slugs as bait 10, 53, *53*
Smooth-hounds 149
Soldier Palmer fly 111, *113*
Sole 157
Specimen hunting 19
Spinning: coarse fishing 42, 44
   sea fishing 177, 182–3, *183*
Spoon lure 44
Spurdog 149–50

Standard wet flies 97, 99–100, *99*, 105–6, 111–17
Steeple cast 79–80
Stewart rig 57
Stickleback as bait 57
Stingray 150
Straddlebug Fly *131*
Streamer pattern fly 100
Sunfish 167
Swannundaze Stonefly nymph *125*
Sweeny Todd lure *120*
Sweetcorn bait 55
Swim-feeders 62

T

Tares as baits 55
Teal Blue and Silver fly *112*
Teeny Nymph *126*
Tench 33, *33*, *36*
Tippets 69–70
Torpedo ray 150
Torsk 154
Trout: brook 81, *81*

brown 81
cut-throat 81, *81*
Dolly Varden 81
rainbow *36*, 81, *94*, *95*
sea 81
steelhead *81*
Tuna *147*, 160, *161*, *194*, *202*
Tunny 160
Turbot 157, *159*

U

Umbrellas 60

V

Vegetable, plants and fruits as bait 55, 56, 57
Vice, fly tying *96*, 97

W

Water knot 76

Watson's Fancy fly *114*
Weevers 167
Wheat bait 55
Whip-finish tool 98
Whisky lure *120*
Whiting 154, 177
Wickhams Fancy dry fly *134*
Wickham's Fancy fly *112*
Williams Favourite fly 111
Woodcock and Green fly *114*
Woolly Bugger lure *118*
Worms as bait 52–3
Wrasse 163, *163*, *179*, *189*
ballan *179*

Y

Yellow Humpy fly *131*
Yellow Matuka lure *118*

Z

Zug Bug nymph *124*
Zulu fly 111, *113*

PICTURE CREDITS

Russell Birkett: pp21; 22; 24 t; 25; 40; 51; 53.

Len Cacutt: pp11tr; 20; 26; 50; 63br; 164; 177; 183t; 185b; 187; 192; 195.

Peter Cockwill: pp94; 95.

Bernard Dreh: p31.

Mike Millman: pp6; 13; 14; 15; 16; 36; 37; 48; 49; 52; 89b; 116; 123; 129; 132; 136; 141b; 142; 143; 144; 148; 152; 153tr; 154; 155; 156; 157; 158; 159; 160; 161; 162; 163; 165; 166; 167; 168; 169; 170; 171; 176; 178tr; 178tl; 179; 180; 181; 182; 185t; 186; 187b; 188; 189; 190; 191; 193; 196b; 197; 198t; 202b; 203.

C. Boyd Pfeiffer: p27.

Al Ristori: pp139; 140; 145; 146; 147; 149; 150; 151; 152; 153c; 183b; 184; 194; 198b; 199; 200; 201; 202t.

Andrew Stuart: pp96; 97; 101; 102; 103; 105; 106; 107; 108; 109; 110; 111; 112; 113; 114; 115; 117; 118; 119; 120; 121; 122; 124; 125; 126; 127; 128; 130; 131; 132; 133; 134; 135.

Ken Whitehead: pp10/11c; 12; 18; 19; 24b; 28; 29; 30; 32; 33; 34; 35; 38; 39; 41; 42; 43; 44; 45; 46; 47; 54/55; 56/57c; 57br; 58; 59; 60; 61; 62/63c; 172; 173; 174; 175.